Take
Part
Art

Take Part Art

Collaborative Art Projects

Bob Gregson

FEARON TEACHER AIDS
Simon & Schuster Supplementary Education Group

To my original research assistants—Terry, Alice, John, Steve, and Brian—and to the newest generation—Matthew, Ryan, Jessica, Robby, Lauren, Alex, Erik, Mike, and Danielle

Special thanks to

• Friend, Dr. F. Peter Swanson for ongoing support
• Teacher Bill Derry for encouragement
• Staff developer Carol Kennedy and teachers of the West Hills School—Peggy Pelley, Marsha Perlmutter, Eileen DeMayo, and Betsy Moakley—for their suggestions, comments, and ideas
• Art teacher Annette Chittenden of Jackie Robinson School for enthusiasm, on-the-spot demonstrations, and ideas—Gremlins, Critters, Multi-Masks, and many more!
• Director Corinne Levin and the Teacher Center of New Haven— an unbeatable resource with unflinching dedication
• Old friend Pat Steier for saving me twenty years ago with Paper Place

Editor: Barbara Armentrout
Copyeditor: Diane Sovljanski
Illustration: Bob Gregson
Design: Diann Abbott

ISBN 0-8224-6781-X

Printed in the United States of America
1. 9 8 7 6 5

Contents

Introduction

The art experience for children is a personal record of experiments and explorations—sort of a diary of development and self-discovery. Traditionally, art is a means of self-expression. Because art gives form to our invisible feelings and ideas, it helps us to define who we are as individuals. The tactile manipulation of art materials provides self-understanding through the hands as well as the mind. Through art, children can discover their own talents and skills.

Everyone has some type of talent. Creativity can be strengthened with a mixture of exposure to new ideas and materials and encouragement to experiment. The projects in this book do not focus on complicated techniques for the sake of impressing others with products, but rather they stress trust in a child's own way of seeing the world. The value of this personal vision is further reinforced as children define themselves within the social context of the group.

Collaborative art balances individual talents with the common goal of the group. Young artists can appreciate one another's differences and similarities in a supportive atmosphere of teamwork. Collaborative art focuses on cooperation rather than competition. Artists work together as equals— pooling resources and complementing different talents to produce a single dynamic project.

Today's artists are not only painters and sculptors. Collaborative art training can also benefit architects, designers, choreographers, set designers, filmmakers, video producers, and advertising executives—and people in many other professions that rely on any sort of creative problem solving. No matter what a person does, the value of communicating abstract ideas is essential. Art is a form of nonverbal communication that is older than writing but just as important.

The Art Teacher

Since art is the reflection of inner feelings, children may be shy about showing their artwork to adults—especially to teachers, who hold such powerful positions in children's lives. Try not to prejudge children's art-work or to compare it with preconceived ideas of what art should look like. Be sensitive to children's limitations, and resist showing them how to do it "better." Enjoy learning along with the children through their own art. The best thing a teacher can do is to stimulate children toward self-learning.

Sometimes a child will not like what he or she has done. This may be due to insecurity or lack of confidence. Reassure the child and reinforce his or her attempts in a positive manner. In art there isn't "right" and "wrong"; there is only personal taste. It is through gentle guidance that children evolve into secure adults. The goal of these art projects is to help children grow into well-rounded adults by developing

- the ability to make choices,
- sensory awareness,
- visual discrimination,
- the ability to define problems,
- the ability to reach creative solutions,
- patience,
- intuition,
- techniques with which to record ideas, and
- a means in which to communicate abstract concepts.

These art projects are designed to stimulate creativity on many levels. The activity descriptions are guidelines that should be freely interpreted so that the activity will engage the enthusiasm of a diverse group.

Motivating the Creative Process

For children, the attitude of the teacher is possibly the most important element in the creative process. Young artists are influenced by what the teacher expects to see. These expectations can interfere with creative problem solving in several ways. Teachers should be aware of cultural and social blocks and should provide a supportive atmosphere for creativity.

Blocks to Creativity

- **Fear of Failure.** Fear of looking stupid, silly, or ignorant often para-lyzes us. No one wants to fail or make a mistake, but doing nothing is probably the biggest mistake of all. We'd never have learned to walk if we were afraid to fall. The teacher can help young artists by encourag-ing them to take a first step—to take a risk. Breaking through our fears isn't easy, and support from a teacher is essential.

- **Need to Conform.** We all want to be accepted as part of the group. To conform to the standard, we dress, talk, and think like everyone else.

Being creative means we are trying something different from the standard solution. Expressing a new idea that runs counter to group opinion can mean disapproval from others. Role stereotyping and gender bias can further inhibit vulnerable girls and boys from crossing boundaries. The teacher must protect children from being afraid to break conventional rules and challenge social conformity.

- **Being Frustrated.** Sometimes we try too hard to be creative. Ideas might not work, and the more we force a solution, the more we fail. When it becomes impossible to solve a problem, the best response is to stop, rest, and relax. The teacher should recognize and respect frustration in young children. Give them time to stop and refresh their creativity.

- **Boredom and Anxiety.** If a problem is boring or doesn't challenge our abilities, it won't spark our creative powers. Conversely, feeling pressured to solve a complex problem can force a superficial solution rather than one that results from an examination of all aspects of the situation. The teacher may need to slow down enthusiastic artists to give them time to think about the best possible solution.

- **Preconceived Judgments.** To come up with the best solution means coming up with a list of ideas and later evaluating them and selecting the best one. When presented with a new idea, our tendency is to point out the flaws. It's easier to defeat an idea than to conceive one. Brainstorming goes against rational, logical, linear thinking; instead, it encourages intuition and free-form, associative thinking. All judgments should be suspended until the flow of ideas has stopped. Creativity is a positive process. The teacher should keep the ideas coming by holding off negative judgments.

- **Lack of Tolerance for Chaos.** Just as a farmer plows a field to rejuvenate the soil with light and air, the creative process stirs things up and can appear disorganized. But eventually ideas will grow and emerge. For those who need order and control, this stage of the creative process can be uncomfortable. This incubation period may be messy, and the teacher will need to tolerate it.

- **Inadequate Definition of the Problem.** Sometimes we limit our solutions because we haven't defined the problems clearly or accurately. A poorly understood problem results in a poorly conceived solution. Computer experts use the term "garbage in, garbage out," which means that if you are working with incorrect information, you will probably get incorrect answers. The teacher should present problems as clearly and thoroughly as possible. Discuss questions with the artists before they begin working.

Sparking Ideas

Being invisible, X-ray vision, floating on a cloud—this book is about creative ideas that motivate personal vision rather than step-by-step techniques. The projects are intended to play along with young artists' need for self-expression; the only ingredients necessary are their personal experiences and abilities. The things that one person sees, hears, knows, and imagines are different from what anyone else sees, hears, knows, and imagines. Because each artist brings his or her own experiences to a project, each project in this book will provide a different experience for each participant.

Many of the activities require that a child add his or her own point of view to a collaborative project. Faced with a blank piece of paper or a ball of clay, the young artist may not know where to begin, because young children are not always aware of the world around them and they do not realize how many things they see and hear every day. It's the role of the teacher or leader to help children understand and remember experiences that can enrich their artwork. Here are a few simple questions (and some possible answers) that may assist memories and add to the flow of creative energy.

What do you see?

A room . . . A bed . . . A table . . . A house . . . A person . . . A friend . . . An enemy . . . A teacher . . . A school . . . A classroom . . . A book . . . A playground . . . A street . . . A bus . . . A truck . . . A car . . . A store . . . A gift . . . A letter . . . A pet . . . A TV show . . . A movie

What do you know?

A hiding place . . . A smell . . . A song . . . A story . . . A game . . . A sound . . . A feeling . . . A sensation . . . A voice . . . A taste . . . A person . . . A book . . . A dog . . . A secret . . . An idea . . . A question . . . An answer . . . A fact . . . A town

What do you imagine?

Being grown up . . . A new house . . . A trip to the moon . . . A ride in a flying saucer . . . A million dollars tax free . . . An elf . . . A giant . . . A castle . . . A witch . . . A monster . . . A scary sound . . . A 10-foot ice cream sundae . . . Being able to fly . . . Being 1 inch tall . . . Being 17 feet tall . . . Being famous . . . Being green . . . Being invisible

Art Materials

Sometimes a mountain of scraps is just the ticket to excite young artists into trying new ideas. In many cases it's the colorful assortment of materials, and not the activity, that ignites possibilities and lights up the imagination. Although basic art supplies are necessary financial investments, many other materials are free for the asking, such as packing materials, industrial scrap, and cardboard cartons. Offbeat art materials force novel solutions and can be the perfect on-the-spot motivator.

Choosing Materials

Having an arsenal of materials on hand can help teachers become inspired. Take time to draw up a list of materials you'd like to have. Send the children on a treasure hunt with paper bags to collect materials. Pass out a list to parents at an open house to let them know what you need; they can be very enthusiastic contributors. Here's a checklist to assist with the collection.

Paper
- Packets of construction paper in assorted colors
- Sheets of white paper in various sizes (at least in $8^1/2$" x 11" and 18" x 24")
- Rolls of white bond or brown wrapping paper, approximately 48" wide
- Newsprint sheets
- Newsprint rolls (ends of rolls can be collected from local newspapers)
- Adding machine rolls
- Waxed paper
- Aluminum foil
- Cellophane or acetate in bright, transparent colors

Cardboard
- Poster board (or oak tag)
- Mat board
- Boxes and cartons

Molding Materials
- Plaster of paris
- Modeling clay

Drawing Materials
- Pencils
- Crayons
- Chalk (thin and thick)

- Felt-tip markers
- Ink

Paint

- Tempera in assorted colors
- Watercolors
- Spray paint

Glue

- White glue
- Paste

Tape

- Masking tape
- Cellophane tape
- Silver duct tape

Equipment

- Brushes in assorted sizes
- Stapler
- Scissors with round ends
- Hole punch
- Steel ruler
- Utility knife
- String
- Rope
- Pushpins

Recycled Items for Equipment

- Old kitchen utensils (for tools to mix and shape clay and plaster)
- Plastic yogurt containers (for paint containers)
- Plastic bowls, cups, and containers (for molds)
- Empty coffee cans (for water containers)
- Aprons and old shirts (for smocks)

Recycled Materials for Art Supplies

- Aluminum foil plates
- Baskets
- Beads
- Bottle tops
- Buttons
- Cardboard boxes and sheets
- Clothing
- Fabric scraps
- Fake flowers
- Fake fruit
- Fake fur
- Feathers
- Leather scraps
- Metallic foils
- Metal scraps
- Mirrors
- Old books
- Old calendars
- Old costume jewelry
- Old magazines
- Old wheels from toys
- Paper towel rolls
- Pompoms
- Ribbon
- Spools
- Sticks
- Stones
- Styrofoam and other types of packing materials
- Styrofoam egg containers
- Tassels and fringe
- Telephone wire
- Toilet paper rolls
- Wallpaper sample books
- Wire
- Wood scraps
- Wrapping paper
- Yarn

Organizing Materials

A permanent art corner is ideal, but it's not always practical. Sometimes art supplies must be stored in a closet and moved into the classroom or other workspace. Use an "art cart" to move selected stored materials into position for an art project. Arrange supplies in boxes, and store them on shelves. Buckets with handles are convenient containers for yarn, fabric, buttons, and loose materials. Label containers so that materials can be easily found.

Setup and Cleanup

An orderly presentation of materials is important because it sends out the message of structure. By setting an example to children, they will understand how to respect art supplies, the room, and other artists as well.

Organize crayons, pencils, scissors, and other small supplies in their own shoe boxes. Store scraps of fabric, cardboard, and paper in large cartons. If materials are organized in their own containers and trays, young artists will learn where to return supplies after they are finished.

Be prepared for the inevitable dirty hands, dripping brushes, spills, and overall mess—and allow time for cleanup. Arrange for the use of a sink, and remember to supply paper towels. Keep mops, rags, and sponges handy. Spread out newspapers to catch splatters, and prepare water-filled buckets to clean paint-clogged brushes. Collect old shirts for smocks—and get ready to roll up your sleeves!

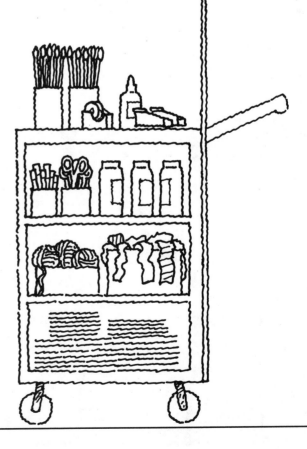

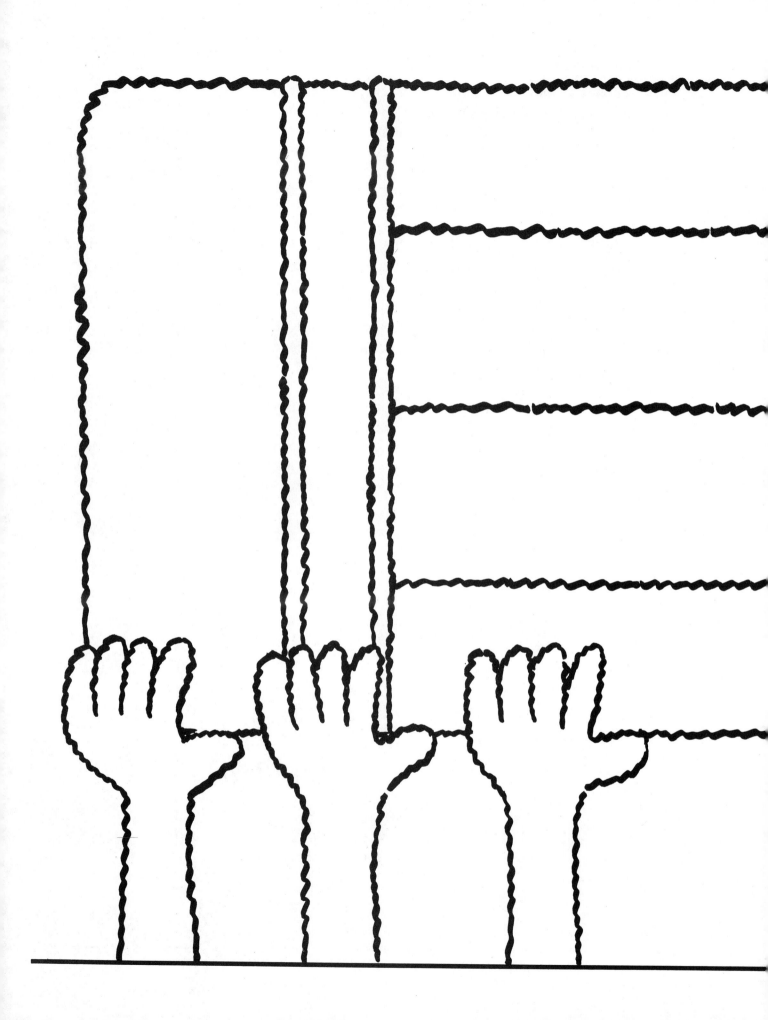

PARTICIPICTURES

Making Memories

We begin collecting memories even before we can remember. As we grow older, we enjoy turning our lives into stories and comparing the imagery of our personal history with that of friends. This group history project is certain to become a memorable moment.

Materials

A large sheet of paper for each artist
Pencils, crayons, felt-tip markers, or other drawing tools

Activity

1. Discuss things that the group has done together. Recall the first time everyone in the group met. How did they feel? Were they afraid, confused, excited, happy? Who did they talk to first? What were they doing when they made friends? What was the first game everyone played together?

2. Give each artist a large sheet of drawing paper and a drawing implement, such as a pencil, a crayon, or a marker.

3. Each artist draws a picture of a memorable experience, possibly including words as well as images. Cartoons are a good way to tell a story. If two artists draw the same experience, it will be fun to see the different versions.

4. Collect the drawings into pages of a book. Have the group arrange them into a story of its history. Make a cover out of heavier paper. Punch holes on the edge and tie the pages together in a book.

5. Have the authors take turns reading and discussing their memories—and maybe even rewriting history.

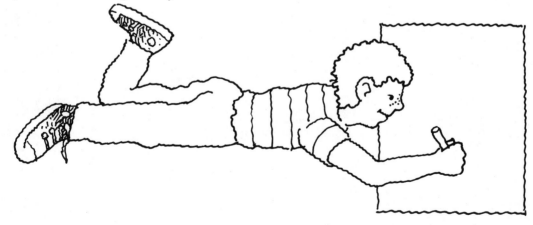

Points of View

We all see things differently. Ask a room of artists to describe the same object or thing, and no two will turn out the same. This project celebrates the diversity of our imaginations.

Materials

A magazine
Felt-tip markers, crayons, or watercolors
Scissors
Glue or tape

Activity

1. Select one picture from a magazine. It can be anything—a person's face, an animal, a scene, or a building.
2. Make enough black and white photocopies to give one to each artist.
3. Along with the photocopy of the picture, give each artist an assortment of art supplies, such as colored markers, watercolors, and crayons.
4. Instruct the artists to change the picture in any manner they wish. For example, they might transform a face into a mosaic with wrinkles of different colors, turn the leaves of a tree into dots of colorful designs, add rainbows to a sky, or cover a building with flowers.
5. After each artist has completed the alteration, hang the pictures side by side and compare the differences. Have the artists react to each other's solutions and enjoy everyone's personal point of view.

Edged Out

Sometimes what's outside the edges of a picture can be more interesting than the picture itself. Artists have an opportunity to explore the areas just beyond the line of vision.

Materials

A magazine, postcard, or photograph
Sheets of 18" x 24" paper
Felt-tip markers, crayons, watercolors, or colored pencils
White glue

Activity

1. Select one photograph, postcard, or magazine picture of a scene, a landscape, or an urban setting. Make an 8$\frac{1}{2}$" x 11" photocopy for each artist.
2. Give each artist a photocopy of the picture, a large sheet of paper, and drawing supplies. The sheet of paper must be larger than the photocopied picture.

 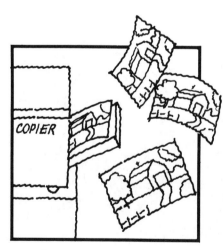 

3. Each artist carefully glues the picture to the center of the paper, leaving enough space around the edges for drawing.
4. Direct the artists to extend the photocopied picture outside the edges onto the sheet of paper. They might begin by continuing horizon lines, walls, streets, and buildings. They can also invent any crazy situation that might be lurking outside the picture. Walls may become wavy, giant flowers may grow through sidewalks, monsters and space creatures may be hiding—anything!
5. Pass around the finished pictures to compare results or to have other artists add another border. Ask the artists if they have suggestions of what might be lurking beyond the edges of the picture they have just finished.

What If?

What would the world be like today if dinosaurs had not been eliminated during the Ice Age or if Thomas Edison had never invented the electric light bulb? Artists can change the course of history, but they must also think about all the other things that would be affected by the change.

Materials

Large sheets of drawing paper for each artist
Pencils
Crayons

Activity

1. Give each artist a piece of paper and a pencil.
2. Discuss important moments in history—Columbus's discovery of America, the invention of the plane, the automobile, and the television, the moon landing, and so forth.
3. Each artist selects a moment in history. The event could be as well known as Charles Lindbergh's flight across the Atlantic Ocean or as unknown (but equally important) as the invention of the transistor.

What would the world be like if the moment in history hadn't happened? In what ways would the world be different today?

4. Each artist draws the world as it might be today if some particular event in history had not happened. For example, if Henry Ford had not invented mass production, everything might still be manufactured slowly, one by one.

5. After the drawings are completed, each artist shows his or her picture to the group. The group takes turns guessing what historic moment has been changed.

Loose Mother Goose

Even Mother Goose might enjoy new twists to age-old nursery rhymes and fairy tales. The cat and the fiddle would sound a little different as a jazz musician with a bass fiddle—but what do you make of that crazy cow jumping over the moon?

Materials

Large sheets of paper
Pencils
Tempera paint, containers, and brushes
Felt-tip markers, crayons, and any other drawing supplies

Activity

1. Divide the group into teams of three or four artists. Give each team a large sheet of paper, pencils, and paints or markers.
2. Write the titles of well-known nursery rhymes and fairy tales on slips of paper. Fold the slips and place them in a box. One person from each team selects a slip from the box. Each team keeps its title secret from the other groups.

3. The idea is to update these familiar stories. Suggest ways in which stories might change, using samples that are not on the slips. For example, Simple Simon might become a pizza delivery boy, or Little Miss Muffet might be watching a horror movie on TV while sitting on a sofa eating a hot-fudge sundae.

4. Each team works together to illustrate the title they have selected. Artists should try not to make the story too obvious. And, of course, they should not include titles on the drawings.

5. After teams have finished their illustrations, display them so that the other teams can try to guess the original stories. Each team gets to tell its new version—hopefully with a happy ending.

Picture Pass

You probably know the old saying about too many cooks spoiling the soup—but is it also true that too many artists spoil the picture? For these cumulative drawings, each artist lends a hand in creating the image. You might say they are drawn from all.

Materials

A sheet of paper for each artist
Felt-tip marker, pencil, or crayon for each artist

Activity

1. Give each artist a sheet of paper and a drawing tool.
2. The artists sit in a circle on the floor or around a table.
3. To begin, each artist draws one simple shape anywhere on the paper— a circle, a square, a triangle, a star, a free-form shape, or anything.
4. After they have each completed a shape, the artists pass their paper to the person on their right. The next artist adds another shape and passes the paper along.
5. The artists continue adding a single shape to each drawing that is passed to them—each time trying to create a recognizable image.
6. Each picture continues around the circle until it returns to the original artist. The artist may add a final shape to help complete the drawing.
7. Each artist shares his or her finished picture with the group—but everyone can share credit for its creation.

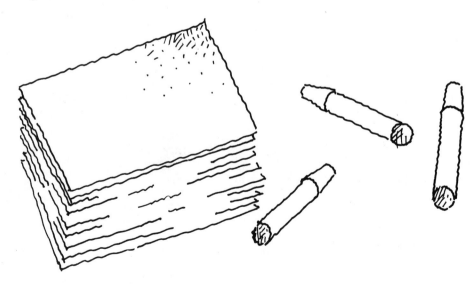

Quick Draw

Is fast art good? Is slow art better? Fast or slow, this is a race that doesn't draw any aesthetic conclusions.

Materials

Chalkboard
Chalk

Activity

1. Divide the group into four teams.
2. Team members line up in back of each other, and each line faces the chalkboard.
3. The first person in each line is given a piece of chalk.
4. At the word "Go!" the first person draws a picture of an object, a person, or a thing.
5. When he or she is finished, the next person is given the chalk and must add something to the object. The artist must draw something recognizable and may not simply scribble a few lines.
6. The chalk is passed along from person to person until everyone in the line has added to the picture.
7. The first team finished may indeed be the winner—but is it art?

Drill Team Drawing

Both dancers and soldiers need lots of practice in order to present those precision steps in unison. Now your young artists will need to rehearse their drill team drawings before they present them to the rest of the group.

Materials

Chalkboard
Chalk
Tape recorder or record player and lively music

Activity

1. Divide the group into teams of three.
2. Select a piece of music for all the teams, or have them select their own.
3. The team members work together to plan a drawing that they can draw in unison to the beat of the music. The drawing must be completed by the last note of the music, and all three artists must draw together as a coordinated team.
4. After practice, the artists are ready to show their stuff. Each team of artists presents its drawing in turn. Everyone can vote for their favorite performance or just give each team a round of applause.

Growth Patterns

Big drawings grow from small shapes as pictures transform before your very eyes. Patterns converge to reveal entirely new shapes.

Materials

Large sheets of paper, approximately 30" x 40"
Pencils
Felt-tip markers, crayons, paints, or other colorful tools (optional)

Activity

1. Divide the group into teams of three artists.
2. Give each artist a pencil, and each team a large sheet of paper.
3. Instruct the artists to draw a very small, simple geometric shape on their team's paper. Suggest that they keep the shapes away from the edges of the paper.
4. Each artist draws another line around his or her shape, following the general contours.

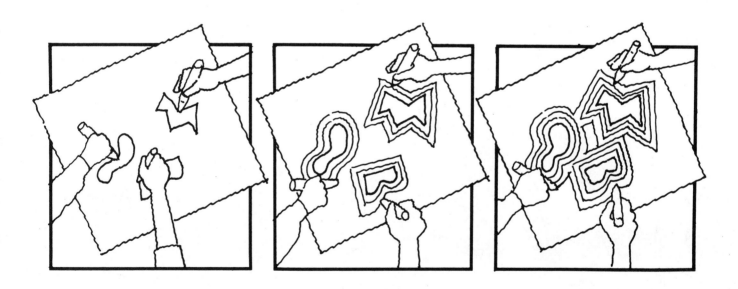

5. The artists continue to outline their shapes concentrically, allowing the shapes to transform themselves into new shapes.

6. When their three shapes converge, the team of artists connects them into one drawing. They continue to outline the shape until the entire sheet is filled.

7. When the papers are completely covered, the teams may want to add color in the outlines with markers, crayons, or paint. The final drawing will appear to have grown into a design on its very own.

Centerpiece

No matter how you slice this project, it still seems to radiate enthusiasm.
The artists create a design from inside out.

Materials

Large sheets of paper or a roll of mural paper
Pencils
Felt-tip markers
Crayons
Tempera paint, brushes, and containers

Activity

1. Divide the group into teams of eight artists. Give each team a large
   sheet of paper or a length of mural paper. Trim the paper into squares.
2. Divide each paper into eight equal wedges in the following manner:

   • fold the paper in half,
   • fold it in half again,
   • unfold the paper to reveal four segments,
   • fold the paper diagonally—corner to corner,
   • fold it again, and then
   • unfold it to reveal eight wedges.

   Finally, trim the paper into a circle so that each wedge is the same
   size.

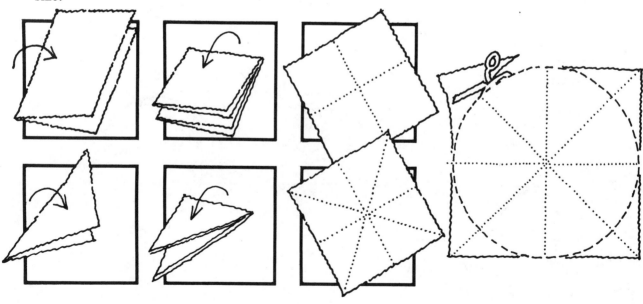

3. To begin, each artist sits or kneels at the end of a wedge. When the leader says "go," each artist begins to draw a design with a pencil, beginning in the center of the paper. The artists must stay within their wedges but must connect their designs with those of the artists on either side. This is not a race, but rather a spontaneous improvisation.

4. It will take some time for the artists to fill their wedges with doodles, dots, lines, and shapes that somehow connect with their neighbors' designs. When the wedges are finished, the artists fill them in with color, using markers, crayons, paint—or all three.

5. The final product will be a mystery until it is hung for all to see—possibly an offbeat kaleidoscope of wacky wedges!

Blotto

The famous psychologist Hermann Rorschach might enjoy these variations on his well-known test. Inkblots come alive as artists discover the hidden personalities within drips of paint.

Materials

A sheet of paper for each person
Tempera paint, containers, and brushes
Felt-tip markers, crayons, and other drawing tools
Scissors
String
A roll of mural paper

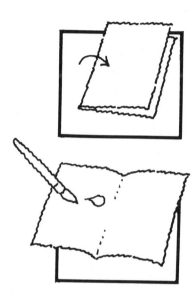

Activity

Variation One: Basic Blotto
1. Give each person a piece of paper.
2. Instruct the artists to fold the paper in half and open it again.
3. They drop some wet paint across the paper in any way they wish.
4. Then they refold the paper, press gently, and carefully reopen it.
5. Let the designs dry. Artists study the designs to allow their imaginations to transform the symmetrical blobs into strange creatures. The designs can be altered with crayons, markers, and paint, and then cut out.
6. Hang the designs from the ceiling, or fill a bulletin board with a world of blotto creatures.

Variation Two: Blotto Pass

1. Give each person a piece of paper.
2. Follow steps 2, 3, and 4 of Basic Blotto; however, each artist drops only a very small amount of paint on the paper.
3. Each artist passes the blot to the next person, who adds another small blob of paint to the paper and folds it again.
4. Continue until everyone has added a small blob of color to each sheet.

Variation Three: Mondo Blotto

1. Take an enormous sheet of mural paper.
2. Have each artist put a few drops of colorful tempera paint on it.
3. Fold the paper in half, and unfold it to reveal the gigantic group blot.
4. Artists then work together to transform the blot into a big blotto being.

Variation Four: Blot Luck

Try folding the paper in different ways to make corner blots, diagonal blots, accordion blots, and so forth.

Headway

It may be hard to believe that the back of the head has its own distinct personality—but it does. Just because we don't see it in the mirror doesn't mean that no one else does. This portrait project might be a hair-raising experience.

Materials

Paper for each artist
Pencils
Pen and ink

Activity

1. Give each person a sheet of paper and a pencil.
2. Instruct each person to draw the back of the head of the person in front of him or her. Suggest that each head be carefully studied for shape and hair style. Artists should try to capture the direction in which hair is brushed, noting braids, ponytails, barrettes, bows, and close-cropped hair. They shouldn't draw collars or clothing because that might give away who the subject is.
3. Final drawings can be completed with pen and ink.
4. Collect the drawings and mix them up. Pass the drawings out randomly. Each person must match up the drawing with the model.

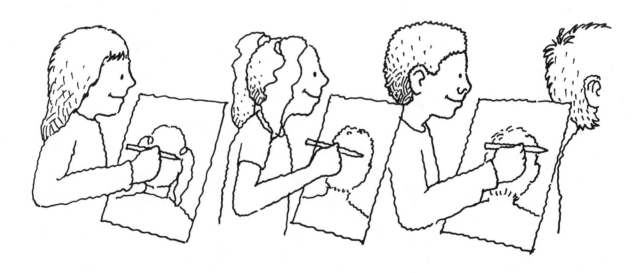

Wall of Fame

We may be unknown today, but we never know what may happen tomorrow. Our egos need not wait any longer! Artists can taste fame on their own terms as they share this exercise in self-promotion.

Materials

Large sheets of paper or poster board
Pencils
Felt-tip markers
Crayons
Tempera paint, containers, and brushes

Activity

1. Each artist makes a list of people whom he or she would like to be. They can be well-known celebrities, TV stars, politicians, or famous scientists—past or present.
2. Give each artist a large sheet of paper or poster board and a pencil.

3. Artists design a poster to advertise themselves as if they were a combination of all the famous people they would like to be. (This is a way to discover individual interests and personalities.) For example, an artist might become a famous Hollywood star who is also a rock musician and a Nobel Prize–winning scientist.

   Direct the artists to

   • pencil in a portrait of how they imagine the celebrity would look,
   • add words to describe the celebrity's incredible talents and how wonderful he or she is, and then
   • fill in the pencil outlines with colorful tempera paint or felt-tip markers.

4. Display the posters on a large wall as a billboard or a "wall of fame." This is a way to introduce the children to each other, or to help them get to know each other better. The group's new-found fame will bring on mobs of fans, autograph hounds, and a lack of privacy—but that's the price of fame!

Funny Money

Some may think that it's rather old-fashioned and not very colorful. It's about time that paper money had a bright, new, up-to-date look! Newly designed money may not be valuable legal tender, but it certainly will be much more fun to use.

Materials

Large sheets of paper
Pencils
Felt-tip markers in assorted colors
Crayons
Watercolors and brushes

Activity

1. Discuss and list the things that group members would like to buy if they had lots of money. The list might include expensive items—such as sports cars, private jets, mansions, trips—or generous gestures, such as making sure everyone has a place to live and food to eat. Allow young artists to fantasize, without judging their selections.
2. Divide the group into teams of two or three people who generally agree on ways to spend their money. Give each team a large sheet of paper, pencils, felt-tip markers, and any other colorful drawing tools that are available.
3. Have the artists examine a real dollar bill. Pass it around for each person to study. Encourage them to notice the way it is designed, with fancy borders, numbers, and the portrait of George Washington on one side and the American eagle on the other.

I SUPPOSE I'M OUT OF A JOB.

4. Discuss ways the bill might be redesigned. The new dollar bill could include some of the same elements, or the shape, size, and images could be totally different. The teams might want to include pictures and symbols of the way they would like to spend money or how money might best benefit all.

5. The teams draw their personal versions of the dollar bill on the large sheets of paper. They might use a second sheet of paper to design the other side of the bill.

6. The teams display their redesigned bills. Each team describes what they will be buying with their money. The group can vote on which one would be the most fun to spend or which would be the best way to spend it. Maybe the Treasury Department might consider using the design—if they pay the designers with the old-fashioned paper money!

Guess-Who Greetings

Greeting cards are an essential part of birthdays and holidays. They are messages of affection from friends and family. The greetings here are anonymous, but they are artistically personalized with the name of the recipient.

Materials

Sheets of paper
Felt-tip markers, crayons, pencils, and other drawing tools
Scissors
Tape
Envelopes

Activity

1. Give each artist a small slip of paper and a pencil. Instruct them to write their name on the paper, fold it, and put it into a small box. Then, one by one, each person picks a secret name out of the box.
2. Next, give each artist a sheet of drawing paper, an envelope, a pair of scissors, and drawing supplies.

3. Instruct the artists to design a greeting card, using the letters of the first name of the person whose slip they picked. Letters may be used as an abstract design or as the basis for a cartoon drawing. Letters have certain expressive characteristics, but it will take a little more invention to create clever designs. Demonstrate this technique to assist artists:

   • Draw the simple shape of an object, person, or thing that may express the name.
   • Divide the shape into the same number of spaces as letters in the name.
   • Fill each space with a letter—altering the letter's shape to conform to the space.
   • Add colors and patterns within the letter shapes.

4. After the artists finish their secret personalized greeting cards, they slip them into envelopes addressed with the person's full name.

5. The envelopes should be placed in a box without any indication of the sender. Distribute the envelopes to the people to whom they are addressed. Card recipients must guess who made their card.

Art-itecture

Legendary architect Frank Lloyd Wright used to call architecture the "mother art" from which all other arts spring. I suppose the idea could be stretched to include almost any aspect of human culture and customs. For now, however, we are not concerned with the practicalities of building but rather with the whimsical invention of design.

Materials

Large sheets of paper
Pencils
Rulers
Felt-tip markers, colored pencils, or crayons

Activity

1. Introduce this project with pictures of great architecture from all over the world. Libraries are filled with books on architecture. For example, the pyramids in Egypt are mostly solid stone with an elaborate maze of corridors and burial chambers hidden within, and the interior of the Guggenheim Museum in New York doesn't have separate floors, but rather one single ramp that spirals up six turns. Investigate the innovative works of famous 20th-century architects—Frank Lloyd Wright, Le Corbusier, Eero Saarinen—and more recent masters, such as Michael Graves and Frank Gehry.

2. Give each young architect a large sheet of drawing paper and an assortment of drawing implements, such as pencils, rulers, and colorful markers. The young architects' assignment is to redesign the room or environment that they are in now—a classroom, camp, recreation center, or living room. The object of this project is to open up new possibilities in architecture.

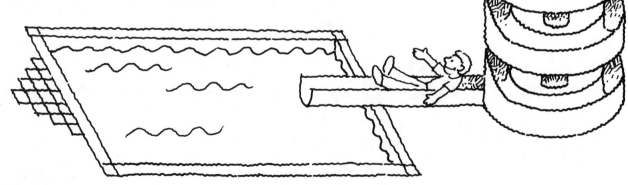

3. This is a fantasy design, so encourage imaginations to run wild. To help architects get started, you should discuss some of the functions of the room—a place to read, a place to play, a place to paint and draw, and so forth. What kinds of things would they like to include? An indoor playground? A secret passage? An ice cream fountain? Anything!

4. Each architect draws a diagram of his or her version of the redesigned room. Plans are playful and need not be precisely measured or accurately represent the actual room.

5. Display the finished drawings for all to see. Which idea appeals to the entire group?

6. Finally, the architects can do an enormous mural that incorporates the best ideas from each design.

   Ambitious architects might even want to build a model out of paper and boxes to try to sell the idea to real estate investors.

Variations

Other architectural projects might include

- the ultimate secret hideaway with an underground amusement park,
- a house for a particular animal, designed especially for its needs, such as a maze for a snake or an ice slide for a penguin,
- a mobile home that might travel anywhere—land or sea—or
- floating architecture.

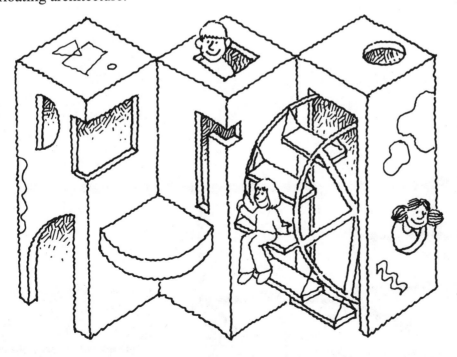

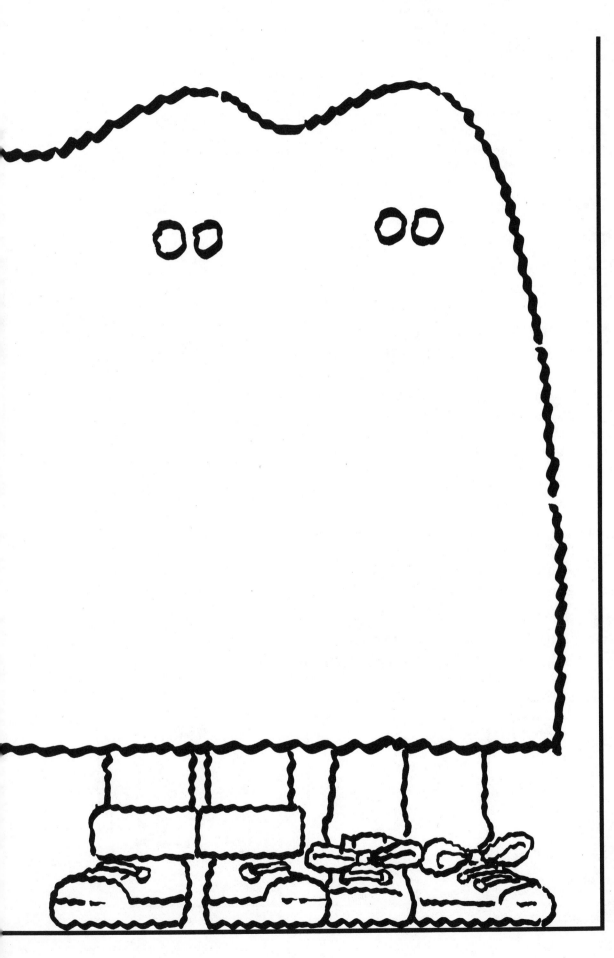

GROUP GARB

Mad Hatters

The concept: three heads are better than one. The challenge: to create a hat that can fit three people at once! Hat styles often bring out one's personality, but these hats will undoubtedly have personalities of their own.

Materials

Sheets of poster board or oak tag
Newspapers
Pencils
Assortment of scrap materials (such as styrofoam pieces, corrugated cardboard pieces, colored paper, sequins, feathers, buttons)
White glue
Stapler
Scissors
Tape
Tempera paint, containers, and brushes

Activity

1. Divide the group into teams of three artists, making sure that team members are approximately the same height.
2. The idea is for each team to create a hat that fits all three members at the same time. Suggest the following headband structure as the basic framework:

   • Each artist cuts a long thin strip of poster board about 3" wide (or takes a double page of newspaper and folds it into a long strip).
   • Each artist wraps the strip around his or her head above the ears and marks the place where the ends overlap.

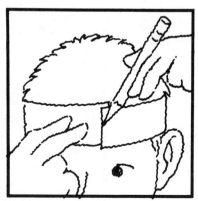 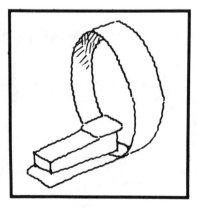 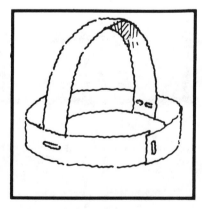

- Each artist removes the headband and staples or tapes it together. The headband should fit securely but comfortably.
- Each team of artists connects their headbands by bridging them with strips of oak tag or folded newspaper and secures the connecting strips with tape or staples.

3. Now each team is ready to begin decorating the top of its hat with a 3-D construction by gluing or taping on scrap materials such as styrofoam, paper, and cardboard.
4. Constructions can be finished with brightly colored paint or special effects such as aluminum foil, sequins, ribbons, buttons, and feathers.
5. When all the hats are finished, each team puts its hat on. Organize a spontaneous hat fashion show, with the teams taking turns modeling their headgear.

    To celebrate, try doing a hat dance—but be careful that teams don't get swelled heads!

Variation

See how many artists can be connected with one hat. Experiment with connecting hats in various configurations. For example, the group might stand in a line behind one another or shoulder to shoulder, in an X-formation, in a circle, or in a random grouping.

Multi-Mask

Artists change their image as they get a new perspective on the world. This project is less a group process than a shared experience. In fact, this is two projects in one: a mask to alter the way others see us and spectacular spectacles to alter the way we see others.

Materials

Oak tag or heavy construction paper for each artist, approximately
   9" x 12"
Colored cellophane
Scraps of yarn
Pencils
Hole punch
Scissors
Tape
White glue
Glitter
Felt-tip markers or crayons

Activity

1. Discuss with the group the different types of images we can express with our faces, such as happy, sad, scary, angry, and friendly. Have each artist decide on an image for a mask.
2. Give each artist a piece of oak tag or heavy construction paper, approximately 9" x 12".

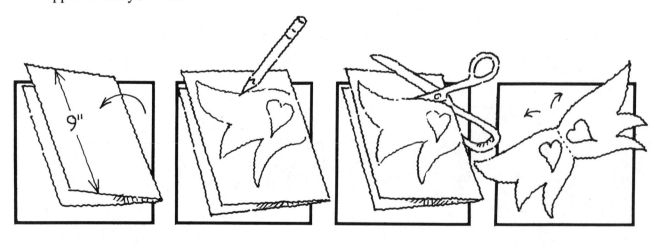

3. Instruct the artists step by step in how to make a mask:

- Fold the sheet of paper in half so that the crease is 9" long.
- With a pencil, draw a free-form shape that expresses the personality of the mask. Be sure to keep the crease as part of the shape.
- Cut out the shape, being careful not to cut off the fold.
- Draw an eyehole of any size and shape.
- Cut the eyehole out of both layers at the same time.
- Unfold the paper to reveal the mask.
- Cut a piece of colored cellophane to fit each eyehole. Some artists like to use a different color for each eye, and others cut strips of several colors for each eyehole.
- Tape or glue the cellophane to the back of the mask.
- Add designs to the front of the mask with markers, crayons, or collage materials. If appropriate for the image to be projected, the designs can be highlighted with lines of white glue sprinkled with glitter.
- Punch a hole in the right and the left sides of the mask, and tie a length of yarn (or ribbon) through each one so that the mask can be tied to the head.

4. When the masks are completed, the artists put them on. Not only will they be expressing their hidden images, but they will also be seeing each other through a new light. Artists might try to describe the way they see things through the colored cellophane lenses, or they might trade masks to share their points of view.

Betwixt and Between

If every ending has a beginning, is there always a middle? Where does the bottom stop and the top begin? These are some of the perplexing problems posed by this people puzzle.

Materials

Roll of mural paper
Scissors
Felt-tip markers
Tempera paint, containers, and brushes
Stapler
Tape

Activity

1. Cut a sheet of paper for each artist. Make it large enough to wear—approximately 5' long. Fold each sheet in half, and cut a semicircle at the folded edge to make a hole that slips over the head.
2. Divide the group into teams of three artists. Make sure the members of each team are approximately the same height.
3. Each team selects something that can be drawn in three parts—front, middle, and end. The image can be an animal, an object, or a person. For example, a horse has a head and front legs, a middle with a saddle, and rear legs and tail. If the team decides to create a picture of a person, make sure that the person can be posed sideways—such as Superman flying or a person lying asleep on the beach.

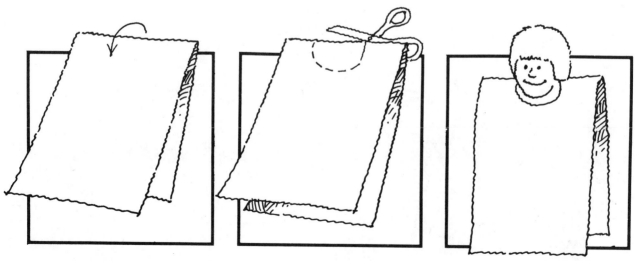

4. After an image is selected, the three artists place their folded sheets of paper flat on the floor, side by side. The artists draw the image across all three sheets, carefully dividing the picture into segments. The artists should work together on all three parts to maintain continuity.

5. When the drawings are finished, the artists put them on and stand next to each other in the correct order, carefully lining up the segments to make a complete picture.

6. Mix up the teams so that the fronts, middles, and ends are rearranged. It may be the only time anyone will see the front of a bus with an elephant middle and a fish tail!

Futuristic Fashions

Fashion designers never stop trying to discover new ways to package people in offbeat styles. Over the years we've worn some pretty strange stuff—from bustles and knickers to miniskirts and Nehru jackets. Now here's a chance for young artists to influence the look of future generations with an exhibit of their own innovative body coverings.

Materials

Roll of mural paper or large sheets of paper
Scissors
Stapler
Tape
Pencils
Felt-tip markers or crayons
Tempera paint, containers, and brushes
Newspapers
Clothesline rope
Clothespins

Activity

1. Discuss and list the types of clothes worn by people in the past and in other countries—for example, knickers, high-topped shoes, kimonos, kilts, and bell-bottom pants. Ask the group to suggest factors that influence clothes design, for example, tradition, fad, and practicality.
2. Divide the group into teams of three. Each design team is to create a model outfit to be displayed in a "Future Fashions" exhibit. Since

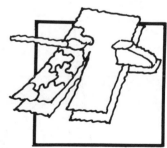

today's fashions are sometimes influenced by yesterday's styles, future fashions might use familiar styles in a new way.

3. Give each design team a large sheet of paper and pencils. All three team members must agree on a single design and

- draw a large outline with pencil of the design;
- fill in the outline with patterns, shapes, and pictures (what will futuristic buttons, zippers, and belts be like?);
- color the garment with tempera paint, felt-tip markers, or crayons;
- cut out the future fashion with a scissors;
- make the back of the garment by tracing the outline onto a second sheet of paper and cutting it out;
- staple the front and back together, leaving one side open;
- stuff crumpled newspaper between the sheets to give the garment a 3-D look; and finally,
- staple the open side closed.

4. Hang the future fashions across the room, clipped to a clothesline, for a World's Fair "Fashions of Tomorrow" display. Design teams may enhance their fashions with a written explanation of the benefits of their new designs.

Variations

As part of a history project, have children research costumes of the past and how they reflected their eras.

Older children might describe the world of the future and the challenges that we will face. Have them design costumes that reflect their predictions.

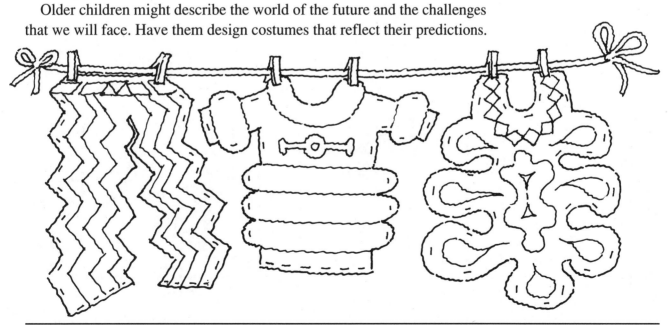

Aliens

Somewhere out in the galaxy there has to be a planet filled with extraterrestrials wondering who we are. The group tries to imagine what our far-out friends might be like and how they might react if they visited Earth.

Materials

Roll of mural paper
Collage materials and scraps
Tempera paint, containers, and brushes
Felt-tip markers
Crayons
Tape
Scissors

Activity

1. Divide the group into pairs. Each pair chooses to come from a different planet in the solar system. (This is a way to learn a little about the solar system and the variations of atmospheres.)
2. Everyone makes a spacesuit to wear when visiting Earth. To make a basic costume, roll out mural paper and cut poncho-sized strips for each artist. Fold each 3- or 4-foot sheet of paper in half, and cut a semicircle into the folded edge for the head to go through. The finished sheet slips over a child's head sandwich-board style, with half in front and half in back.

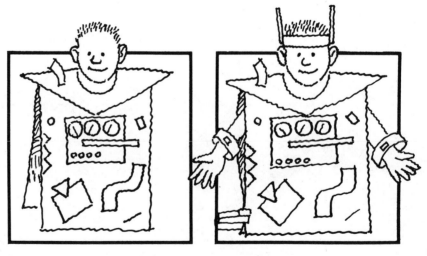

3. Artists alter their ponchos with paint, scissors, and collage materials. The idea is to make a costume of a visitor from another planet who has just landed on Earth. Costumes might include a voice translator (to communicate in Earth languages), an air changer (to breathe our atmosphere), and a vision sensor (to be able to see the same colors and shapes that humans do).

4. When the costumes are completed, each pair begins its mission. Alien pairs roam around Earth to check out the planet. Give each pair of extraterrestrials paper and pencils so that they can take notes as they observe Earthlings and their habits. Lists might include the following observations.

   • **Earth greetings:** Shaking hands, bowing, tipping hats (men only), saying "How are you?," waving, kissing
   • **Earth food:** Three different meals a day, eaten with knives, forks, and spoons (some earthlings use two sticks called chopsticks); eating exploded kernels of corn (called popcorn) in a darkened room with lighted pictures (called movies)
   • **Earth costumes:** Men wear a piece of fabric around their neck (called a tie), women prop up the back of their feet with sticks (called high heels), men put white bubbles on their face and slice off little hairs (called shaving), and women color their mouth with a crayon (called lipstick)

5. After each pair of extraterrestrials has completed its exploration, everyone returns to the home star and reports on the wonders of Earth. One by one, each pair of aliens tells of the strange customs of Earth's inhabitants.

Camouflage

During war, battleships are painted to blend into water and sky, tanks are covered with blotches of green, brown, and black to blend into the landscape, and soldiers wear leaves and branches on their helmets to blend into trees and bushes. In this project artists try not to stand out as they invent ways to fade into their surroundings.

Materials

Roll of mural paper
Cardboard boxes
Tempera paint, containers, and brushes
Pencils
Scissors
Utility knife
Tape

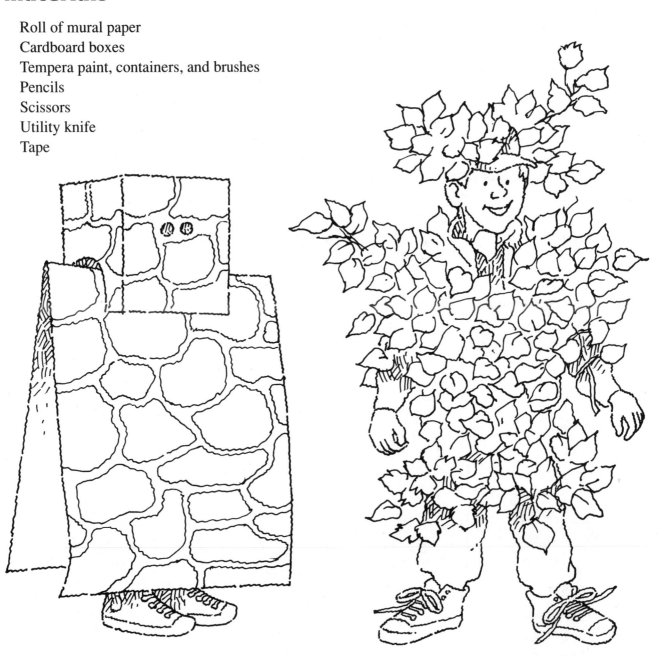

Activity

1. The goal is to create inconspicuous costumes that blend into the background so that the entire group disappears!

   Divide the group into teams of three to five. Each team selects a background to blend into, such as a woods, bushes, a stone wall, a fence, or a door. Blending into foliage is easier, but architectural backgrounds are a challenge for inventive minds.

2. After choosing a background, each team designs "invisible" costumes. Here are some ideas for techniques.

   • **Trees and Bushes:** Wear dull green or brown pants and shirt. Wrap twigs and leaves around legs and arms, and tie them with string.
   • **Buildings, Fences, and Walls:** Cut out a paper poncho from a long piece of mural paper. Paint it to look like bricks, stones, wooden slats, or whatever the design may be.
   • **Hideaways:** Create an object that would seem naturally at home in any setting, such as a mail box, a trash container, a planter, or a sign. Use a large cardboard box as the basis for a team hideaway.

3. After the camouflage costumes are finished, the teams test them out. Teams that cannot be found get a cheer from the rest of the group—unless they never appear again!

Together We Stand

For centuries the centerpiece of traditional Chinese celebrations has been the dragon costume worn by dozens—or hundreds—of people. Group spirit fills this collective costume as everyone becomes a single character.

Materials

Large cardboard box
Bolt of fabric
Tempera paint, containers, and brushes
Utility knife
Scissors
Tape
Scrap materials
Spray paint

Activity

1. The group decides on the character it would like to become—a dragon, a snake, a bird, an octopus, or whatever—something large enough to include the entire group.
2. Lay out the materials to build the creature. Use a cardboard box for the head, a long roll of fabric for the body, and cardboard scraps and other recycled materials for wings, arms, tail, and any other surface decoration.
3. Divide the group into three teams of three to five artists each. One team works on creating the head, another team produces the body, and the third creates any additional special details.

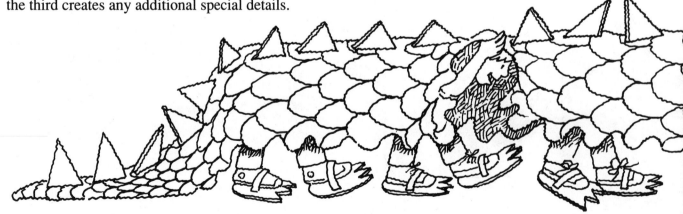

4. The "head team" can create a wide mouth (with or without teeth) by cutting through the box with a utility knife. Eyes, ears, nose, teeth or beak, and other details can be painted or constructed from scrap materials.

5. The "body team" paints the fabric body, using tempera paint and brushes or spray paint. Designs and patterns can be swirled over the entire fabric. It can also add textured details such as feathers, fins, and scales.

6. The "details team" creates all the special effects that bring the creature to life. This team might make webbed feet, paws, wings, or tentacles, and even noisemakers to add to the theatrics. These details can be constructed from whatever scrap materials are handy.

7. After each team has completed its section, the group connects them. Have the group rehearse walking, undulating, and shaking in unison to give the illusion that it is one big creature. When the group has learned to synchronize its movements, let the creature take a stroll—and watch the reactions!

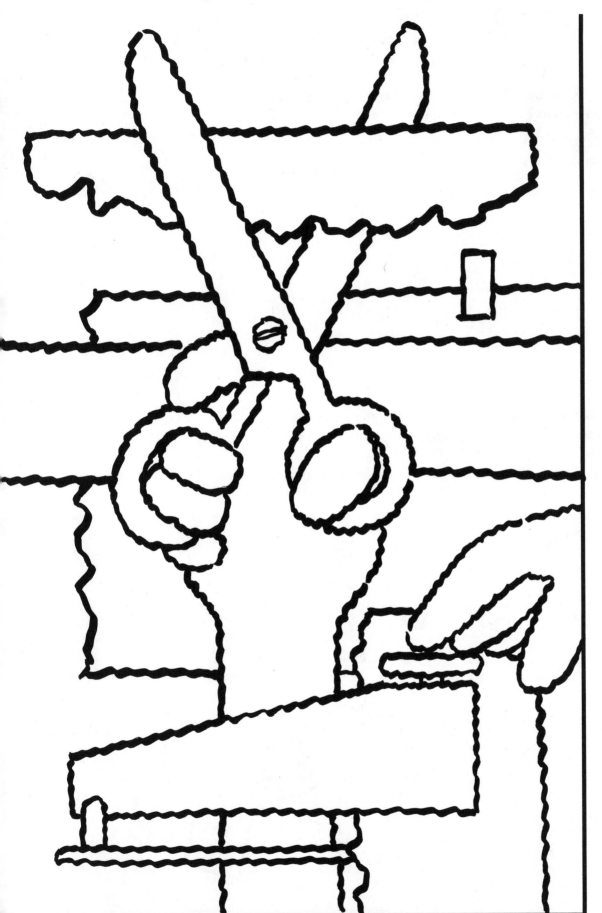

COLLABORACOLLLAGE

Opposing Forces

This collage may seem more like a collision of tastes as two artists produce a picture in which opposites not only attract but must also be attractive.

Materials

Magazines with lots of photographs
Colored paper
Large sheets of paper
Scissors
White glue
Cellophane tape

Activity

1. Discuss the idea of opposites—good and bad, high and low, big and small, dark and light, rich and poor, ugly and beautiful, and so forth.
2. Divide the artists into pairs.
3. Give each pair a large sheet of paper, scissors, white glue, and some magazines.

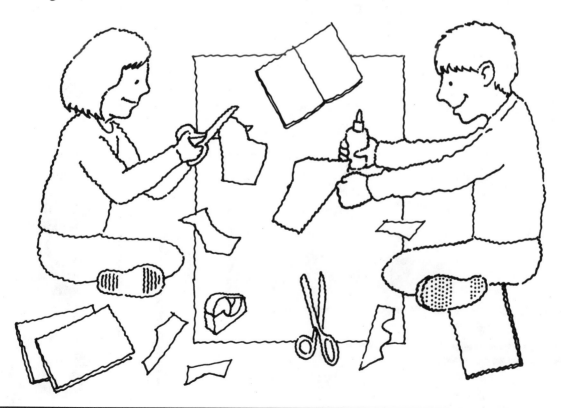

4. The idea is to make a collage that includes as many opposites as possible. The two artists independently select a magazine picture to place in the collage. Then they each must find a picture that reflects the opposite of the one their partner selected. For example, one artist selects a rainy scene and the other selects a picture of a fancy dinner. Then each must find the opposite of the other's picture—perhaps a sunny scene and a picture of a fast-food burger.

5. The goal is for the pair of artists to create a collage in which opposites seem to exist naturally together on the same piece of paper.

Hearsay

The Sunday comics originated them. Artist Roy Lichtenstein turned them into pop art. Undoubtedly, this project will add another chapter to the ongoing development of the cartoon strip.

Materials

Magazines with lots of pictures
Scissors
Roll of mural paper
White glue
Cellophane tape
Felt-tip markers

Activity

1. Roll out the mural paper on the floor.
2. Artists begin to cut out magazine pictures of people in different poses and situations—sitting, standing, lying, talking, walking, and so forth. The pictures can be full figures or only head and shoulders.
3. Next, they cut out headlines, phrases, and sentences from magazine stories or advertisements. Advertisements are ideal for this activity because they usually have concise copy printed in a simple, bold type-face.

4. The artists glue the pictures into an enormous scene on the roll of paper. Larger images can form the foreground, and smaller images can look like they are in the distant background. Buildings, furniture, walls, trees, or any other settings can be drawn around the figures to tie the composition together.

5. Finally, the artists match the headlines and quotes with the pictures of people. Words are glued over the heads of the people and enclosed in cartoon "balloons" (drawn with a felt-tip marker) as if the people were speaking the words.

Variation

Have the artists create a play from the random quotes by arranging them into a script.

Window Collage

Windows will be looked at instead of through when the sun turns them into a colorful light show. The project is based on stained glass windows, but the results are purely the artists' own.

Materials

Sheets of medium-weight colored acetate (a roll is less expensive than precut sheets)
Scissors
Cellophane tape
Hole punches
Self-stick labels

Activity

1. Arrange the art supplies in the center of the work table.
2. Have artists suggest themes for the window collages. They might be inspired to do an underwater scene with fish and seaweed; a sky scene with birds, planes, and clouds; a fairy tale scene with a castle; or a colorful abstract composition of shapes.
3. Divide the artists into groups of three to five for each theme. They can cut out simple shapes from the acetate; more complicated shapes should be drawn with felt-tip markers or ballpoint pens before being cut out. Circles can be traced from plates or lids. Textures and patterns can be added with the hole punch or with self-stick labels of various colors and shapes.

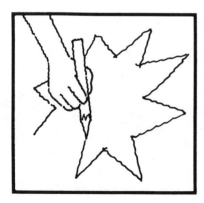 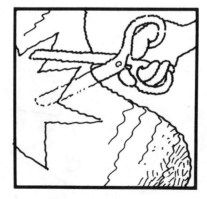 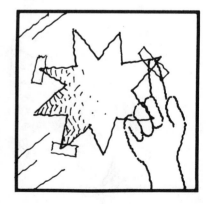

4. Because acetate will stick to itself, the artists can rub acetate shapes together to make the design. The artists will have fun blending colors by overlaying one transparent color over another to make a third color. Clear cellophane tape will be necessary to attach the designs to the window.
5. Give the artists plenty of time to explore how the light in the room is transformed by the colorful window collages.

    Window collages are most dramatic when the glass is completely filled with color—and of course, when the sun is out.

Light Sight

With only a slight alteration, flashlights make miniature light shows. I suppose you could say that artists are guaranteed a creative flash.

Materials

Common hand-held flashlights (supplied by the artists)
Black construction paper
Clear acetate or cellophane
Pencils
Scissors
Masking tape
Felt-tip markers
Hole punches
X-acto knife

Activity

1. Each artist brings in a hand-held battery-powered flashlight.
2. Give each artist a sheet of black construction paper. The artists can share scissors, pencils, hole punches, markers, X-acto knives, tape, and other supplies.

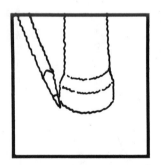 

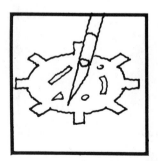  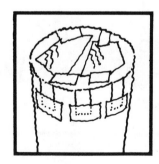

3. To turn the flashlights into light-show spotlights, instruct the artists to

- place the bulb end of the flashlight on the black paper and trace around it with a pencil;
- add tabs to the circle and then cut it out with scissors;
- cut three to five tiny holes of various shapes, such as a triangle, slit, or zigzag, into the black circle (use an X-acto knife for straight-edged holes and a hole punch for round holes);
- place the black circle over the bulb end of the flashlight, and tape the tabs to the sides; and finally,
- cut a small piece of clear acetate to fit over the black paper, tape it on, and color the acetate over the holes with markers (or tape pieces of colored cellophane over the holes).

4. Darken the room as much as possible (or find a room without windows) and have all the artists turn on their flashlights. Experiment with changing designs by having them move their lights back and forth and closer and farther to the walls and ceiling. Add music and have the artists choreograph their movements into a unified light dance.

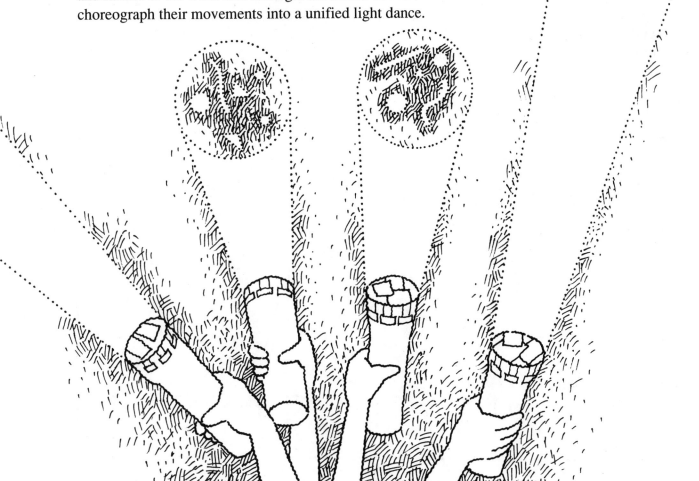

Framework

Sometimes it's the frame that turns an ordinary picture into a work of art. These frames will transform anything into a work of art, and any place into an art show.

Materials

Poster board or sheets of cardboard
Scissors
Utility knife
Tempera paint, containers, and brushes
Crayons, felt-tip markers, pencils, and other drawing tools
String

Activity

1. The idea is to turn the room into an art exhibit. Give each artist a sheet of cardboard. Set out tempera paints, crayons, scissors, and other art supplies for all to share.
2. Instruct each artist to cut out a rectangular hole in the center of the poster board or cardboard. The size of the hole will determine the size of the frame. Adult supervision will be necessary if the artists use utility knives or other sharp cutting tools.
3. The artists decorate the frames with designs such as stars, flowers, hearts, shapes, and squiggles. They can also trim around the outer edge of the frames to give them unusual shapes. The final step is to punch two small holes at the top of each frame and tie a length of string through them.

4. The artists each search the room for something to frame. Encourage them to work together to find or arrange interesting compositions. The frames can be hung in front of bookcases, desks, plants, windows, or any other object. Use existing hooks, or tape the frames up.

5. Arrange a special art opening for the exhibit. The artists can dress up in arty outfits—with sunglasses and berets, for instance. At the opening party, artists get to see their everyday world in new ways—and discuss the lofty ideas behind their creations.

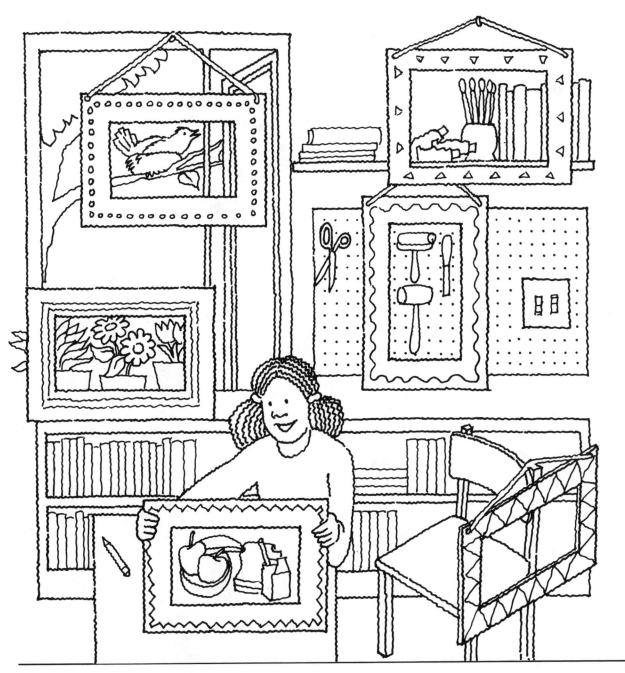

Made Anew

Found objects that have outlived their usefulness are recycled for a
second chance and a totally different existence.

Materials

Discarded objects, such as toys, clocks, small furniture, and utensils
White glue or contact cement
Spray paint
Silver duct tape
Tools, such as a hammer, a saw, and a screwdriver

Activity

1. Each artist selects a discarded object that has many parts and can be
   easily dismantled, such as an old plastic toy, a radio, or a clock.
2. The artists carefully cut or break their object into as many pieces as
   possible. Discourage overenthusiastic destruction that might harm
   someone. Encourage artists to think about how the object might be
   dismantled and what shapes will look best.

3. Each artist reassembles his or her object in a totally new way. The object's former existence can be disguised by rearranging the pieces into an entirely different shape and attaching them with white glue or contact cement. Pieces might also be spray-painted before or after they are assembled to change them even more.

Variation

The artists might connect their newly assembled objects into one gigantic sculpture. Or individual artists may want to exchange pieces for totally new assemblages.

Fantasy Furniture

Many architects and artists have created unusual furniture designs. Some of their chairs look like they belong in a science fiction film, and others look like animals or flowers. Now, young artists get the chance to redesign their immediate reality into an unreal one.

Materials

Corrugated cardboard
Paper
Scissors
Jigsaw
Tempera paint, brushes, and containers
Crayons
Tape
String

Activity

1. Artists share supplies of paper, cardboard, paint, tape, and so forth.
2. Artists work together to redesign the furniture in the room. The function of the furniture must not change—a chair must still be able to be sat on—but the shape and style of the furniture should become totally different.
3. Furniture may be covered with paper, cardboard, or scraps of fabric to hide its shape and change it into a new fantasy. Changes are temporary, so care should be taken not to mark up the furniture or damage it in any way.
4. Artists neatly paint designs on the new surfaces. Pictures of people may inhabit the new chairs, and tables may be covered with odd-sized objects or disguised as flowering bushes.

Perplexing Puppets

Get ready to enter another dimension of puppetry: abstract puppets.
Puppet creatures begin to appear before our eyes, as teams of artists
decide what their puppet personalities will reveal.

Materials

Poster board and oak tag
Pencils
Scissors
Tempera paint, containers, and brushes
Felt-tip markers
Collage materials, such as paper cups, yarn, egg cartons, and foil
White glue
Tape
Paper fasteners
Dowels

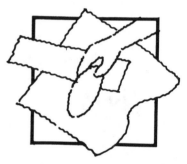

Activity

1. Divide the group into pairs. Give each pair a sheet of poster board, a
   pencil, and a scissors.
2. Ask each artist to draw two shapes on the poster board with a pencil.
   The shapes can be of any size and design—long, thin, fat, round,
   squiggly, pointy. The result is four odd abstract shapes on each poster
   board.

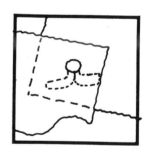

3. The artists cut the shapes apart with a scissors. Have the pairs place their shapes together in different configurations. Ask them to think about what the configurations might resemble—a person, a monster, a prehistoric animal, a space alien, a weird bird? The pairs rearrange their shapes, turning them upside down and flipping them over for various points of view.

4. Both artists decide what their abstract puppet creature will be. They hinge the shapes together with paper fasteners to connect arms and legs to bodies. Artists may want to make additional shapes out of poster board and hinge them on to enhance the variety of movement.

5. Then they add 3-D collage textures to the surface of the puppet. Paper cups, yarn, egg cartons, foil, and other scrap materials from the resource box can become eyes, fins, ears, hair, and other details.

6. To assist with movement and presentation of the puppet, the artists tape long dowels on the back.

When a pair of artists have completed their collaborative creation, they can develop a voice and character to express the puppet's unique personality. They can also construct colorful abstract scenery to make the puppets feel right at home in their offbeat world.

Quick-Built Quilt

This patchwork project is an old-time quilting bee with up-to-date themes.

Materials

White glue
Scissors
Sewing machine
Colorful pieces of felt

Activity

1. Give each artist a piece of dark-colored felt, approximately 10" x 10", as a background for his or her quilt patch. Also supply the artists with pencils and paper.
2. The theme of the quilt is "favorites." Each artist picks his or her favorite thing to illustrate on the patch—food, flower, sport, TV show, animal, or anything.
3. Each artist draws his or her favorite thing on a piece of paper. Since felt is not a good medium for intricate detail, encourage artists to simplify the drawings to basic shapes.

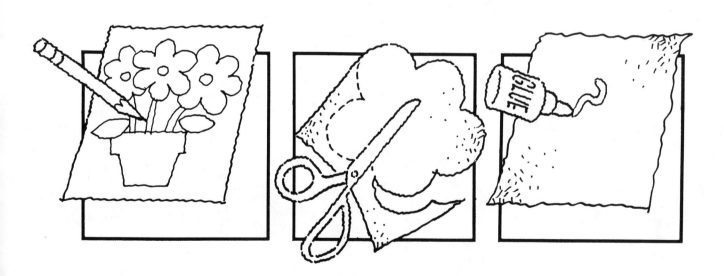

4. Using the drawing as a pattern, each artist cuts out colored felt shapes and places them on the background. It's best to begin with larger shapes, such as rectangular buildings, curvy hills, and oval faces. Add smaller details, such as windows, trees, and eyes, on top of the larger shapes.
5. The artists attach the pieces of felt with dabs of white glue. Let the patches dry thoroughly.
6. Pin or sew each 10-inch patch into one enormous quilt. Begin by sewing patches into rows, and then sew the rows together. The artists will agree that the result is a real "crazy quilt."

Web Weaving

Artists will unwind as they get tangled up in this intriguing web.

Materials

String
Yarn
Rope
An assortment of scrap materials, such as feathers, sticks, cardboard,
    foil, and paper
Scissors
Tape
White glue
Tempera paint, containers, and brushes

Activity

1. Designate a place in which to construct the web—for example, among
   the backs of several chairs or a cluster of trees or throughout an entire
   room, filling it back and forth from wall to wall.

2. The group works together, running string from point to point until it begins to resemble a gigantic web. Areas of the web structure can be tied into shapes by pulling several strands together. Suggest that the artists incorporate thick and thin string and yarns of various colors to make the web "lines" visually varied—like a drawing in space.

3. After the web has been constructed, the artists can suspend colorful shapes and objects within it. Colored paper shapes, painted sticks and twigs, feathers, buttons, and other found objects can be attached until the web appears solid with tiny artworks.

   The result will be a 3-D collage that will impress any spider!

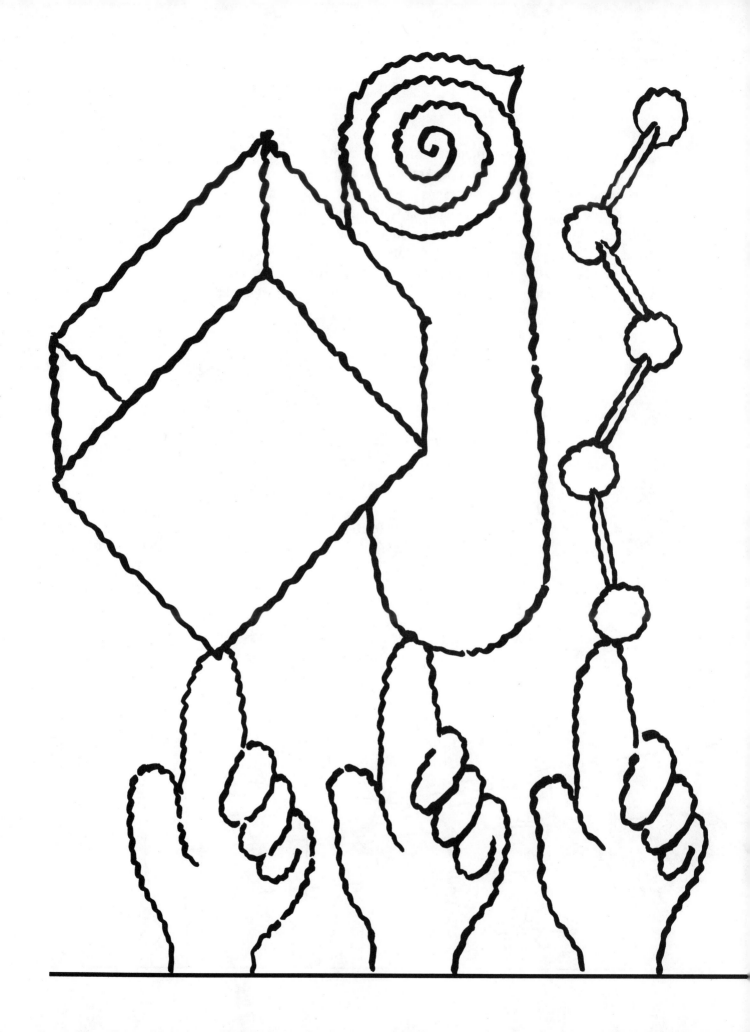

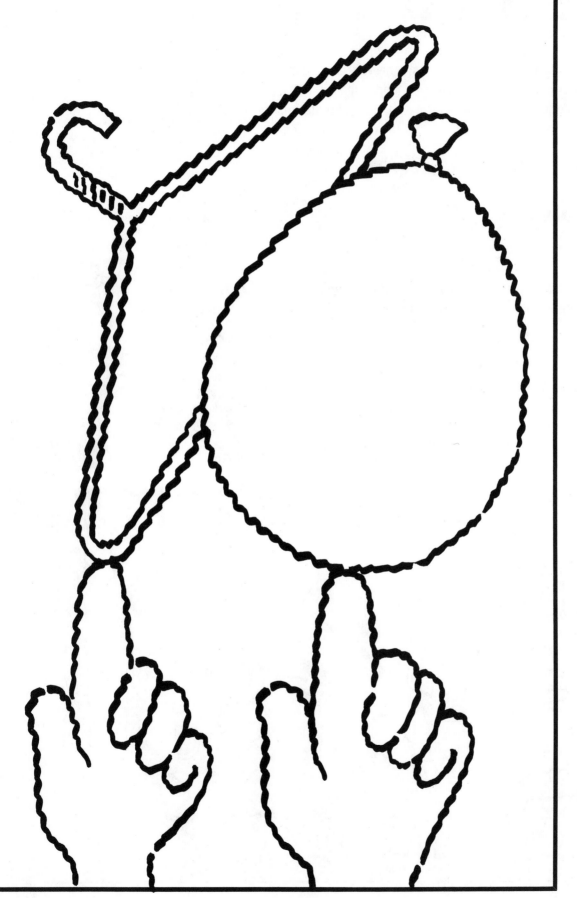

SCULPTURE SQUAD

Sticks and Stones

Long before fancy art supplies were invented, primitive civilizations expressed themselves with anything at hand, such as sticks, stones, mud, and leaves. Today, in our industrial world, natural materials may be harder to find than man-made ones, but the challenge of expression still exists.

Materials

Stones of various sizes and shapes
Branches and limbs
Small natural objects, such as leaves and feathers
Tempera paint, brushes, and containers
String
Yarn
Scissors
Colored construction paper
Stapler

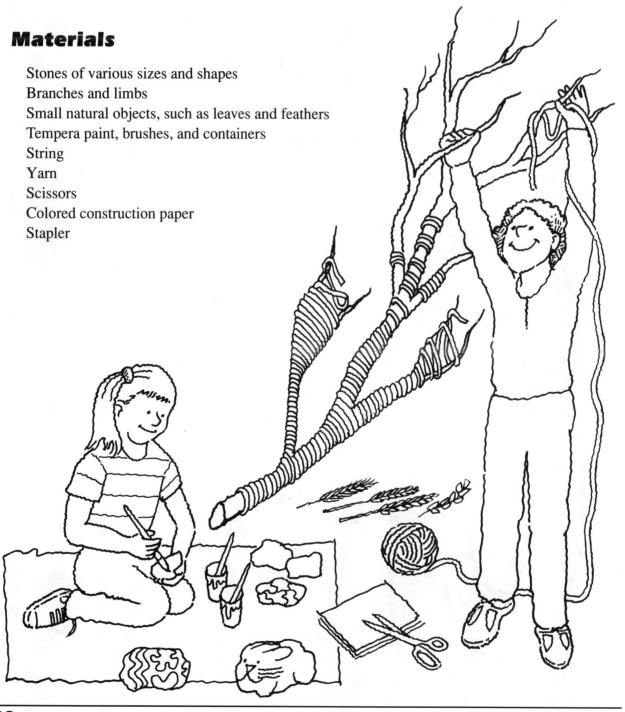

Activity

1. Place all materials in the center of an open space. Cover the floor with paper so that you won't have to clean up paint and litter later.
2. The idea is to build an environment with natural materials. Young artists twist and tie branches into shapes. Form an intricate web of branches by having the artists connect them.
3. They can decorate the branches with paint or maybe wrap them with various colors of yarn or fabric. Yarn can be woven back and forth throughout the branches, while leaves, feathers, and other materials can be inserted and tied on.
4. Have artists study the shapes of the stones. Suggest that they paint designs on the stones, following the natural contours of the surfaces. The shape of a stone may suggest a particular image, animal, or abstract design.
5. Display the stones with the branch sculptures or tie them on with string. Smaller stones might be woven directly into the yarn.

   As a follow-up to this project, the artists might like to explore primitive civilizations or American Indians to see how artworks compare.

Toothpick Trick

The versatile toothpick is the basic building material for this sweet-tooth sculpture. This project is easy to stick to because it's fast and there are no mistakes!

Materials

Toothpicks (the round cocktail ones are best)
Miniature marshmallows
Gumdrops

Activity

1. The construction technique is simple. Toothpicks are used as construction beams with marshmallows or gumdrops as connectors. (Dried peas work well, too, if you soak them overnight first.)
2. Since the construction is so fast, take a few minutes to discuss ideas with the group. Triangular shapes are sturdiest, so geometric forms or

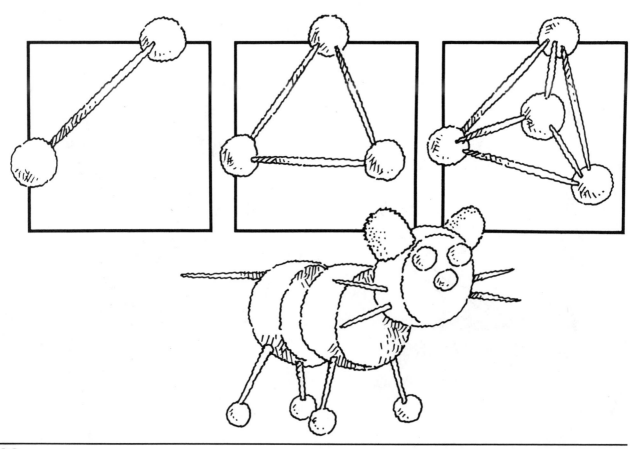

geodesic domes are great ideas to try. Artists might want to experiment with abstract forms or create robots, animals, or even a model of the Eiffel Tower.

3. Encourage a group project, or divide toothpicks and connectors evenly among artists and see what each person comes up with. For a grand finale, connect the individual projects to form one gigantic toothpick triumph.

Hanger Up

Have you ever noticed how wire hangers seem to mysteriously multiply in the closet? Extra hangers will have a second career as the basic structure of this high-wire act.

Materials

Lots of wire hangers
Silver duct tape or adhesive tape
Paper towels
Liquid starch
Disposable aluminum pie tins
Spray paint
String
Newspaper

Activity

1. Give each artist about six wire hangers.
2. Artists twist and bend hangers into shapes. To begin, they can bend the hanger's "shoulders" together or pull the bottom down to make a diamond shape.

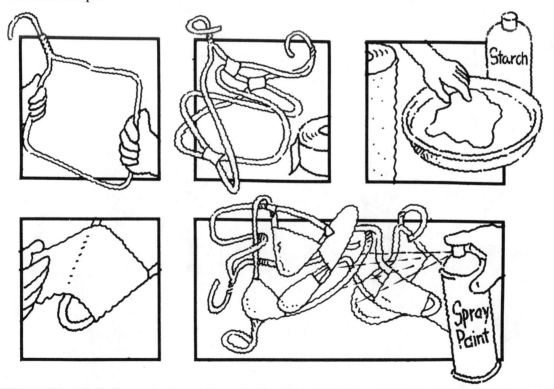

3. The artists connect their first two hangers with strips of silver duct tape or adhesive tape, intertwining the wires as much as possible. They continue to connect their other four hangers, trying to keep the hooks within the center of the sculpture. Suggest that they turn the sculpture until it looks balanced from all angles.

4. When the wire frameworks are finished, the artists tear paper towel sheets in 6-inch-wide strips and soak them in the disposable pie tins filled with liquid starch. The paper towel strips should be kept as flat as possible.

5. The artists carefully lift the paper towel strips from the pie tins and remove the excess starch with the edge of a finger. They stretch each strip between two sections of wire, wrapping the ends around the wire to securely attach them. This is continued until the wire structure is filled with paper—leaving some spaces to see through. Newspaper should be placed under the sculpture to catch the drips.

6. When the starch has dried thoroughly, the sculptures can be sprayed with metallic silver or gold paint or with paint in bright primary colors.

7. With more tape, the artists can join their sculptures. Suspend the sculptures from ceiling fixtures with string to create a wire cloud of frolicking shapes.

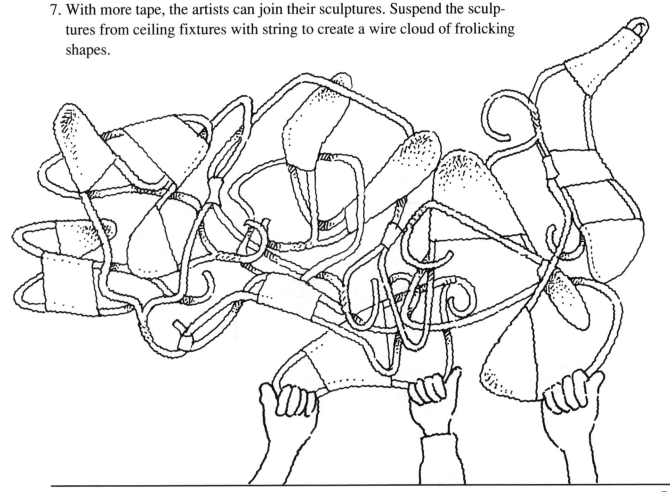

Moonscapes

These string things resemble a see-through surface of the moon, but these lunar sculptures aren't as loony as they sound.

Materials

Balloons of various sizes and shapes
String and yarn
White glue or liquid starch
Disposable bowls

Activity

1. Instruct each artist to blow up a balloon and tie it.
2. Fill the disposable bowls with liquid starch or white glue (add a small amount of water to keep the glue thin).
3. The artists immerse pieces of string or yarn into the glue. Because yarn absorbs more glue than string does, they will have to gently squeeze out the extra liquid from the yarn.

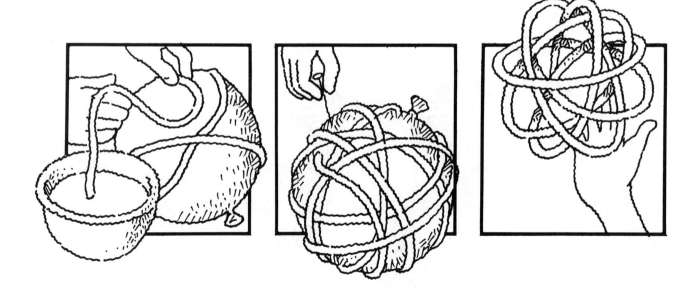

4. The string or yarn is wrapped around the balloon. Artists twist it into various patterns and designs like the surface formations of the moon.

5. After the balloons are each covered with a crisscross lunar landscape, allow them to dry for a few days. Tie a string to the knot of each balloon and hang them up—away from the curiosity of anxious fingers.

6. After the sculptures are absolutely dry, pop the balloons with a pin and very carefully remove the balloon pieces. The string things can then be sprayed with paint or patiently painted with tempera and small brushes.

7. When all the moons are completed, the group designs a constellation of moonscapes. The group can create a mural backdrop with stars and other space symbols and suspend the moons in front of it with strings from the ceiling. To complete this stellar show, aim a spotlight or flashlights at the mysterious shapes.

Paper Place

Paper is an easily conquered sculptural material. Just cut, twist, and staple and you've got an instant form. If you add forms to forms, the paper sculpture will quickly grow until these innocent two-dimensional sheets consume the three-dimensional space of the room.

Materials

Lots of paper—construction paper, leftover copier sheets, and so forth
Scissors
Staplers
Hole punches
Cellophane tape
String

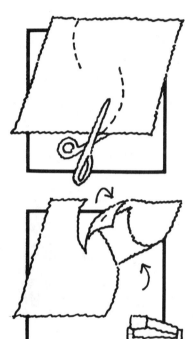

Activity

1. Before beginning the activity, set up the room. Run string back and forth across the room low enough to be reached by small artists. Place scissors, hole punches, staplers, cellophane tape, and a pile of paper in the center of the room. Keep stapler refills handy.
2. Introduce the basic paper-sculpture vocabulary to the artists by demonstrating this simple technique:

- Cut two or three random slits into a sheet of paper.
- Twist a piece of the paper forward, curling it into a shape, and staple.
- Twist another piece backward, curling it into another shape, and staple.
- Twist each remaining piece into a shape and secure it with a staple.
- Fringe an edge with small, repeated cuts.

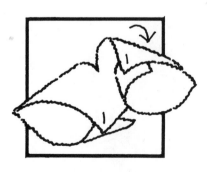

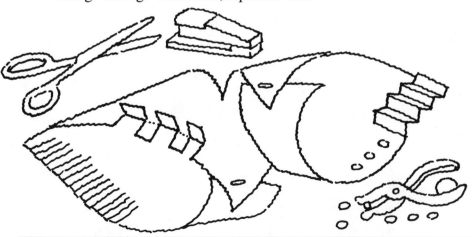

- Make a pleat by cutting a strip of paper and folding it back and forth.
- Add a few holes with the hole punch for texture and pattern.
- Take another sheet of paper and repeat.
- Attach both abstract paper forms together with a stapler to create a larger shape.

3. Divide the group into teams of two or three artists. Each team makes a paper sculpture by connecting many shapes into one large shape—for example, a long row of connected forms that stretches from wall to wall or a huge ball of flowering shapes that reaches from floor to ceiling.

4. The artists experiment with as many techniques as possible. Paper sculpture is a popular art form, and libraries have many books on various examples. For instance, cut a spiral, starting in the center of a sheet of paper, and watch it expand into a single ribbon. And paper chains are familiar to most children. How many other ways can strips of paper be looped and connected? Fold paper into shapes, cut, and open the paper to reveal new forms.

5. Urge the artists to continue until the room is completely filled with shapes.

   Exhausted artists may want to sit within or lie underneath the paper environment to admire the transformation—a perfect time for a quiet game or for thoughts about the next art project.

In the Bag

Sssh! No one knows what's up because artists produce their artwork under cover.

Materials

Grocery bag for each artist
An assortment of art supplies, such as paper, crayons, felt-tip markers, and modeling clay

Activity

1. Fill the paper bags with simple art supplies that will fit into a bag, such as paper, crayons, modeling clay, and anything else at hand.
2. Give each artist a paper bag. Instruct the artists to look inside their bags and figure out how to use the art supplies to make a secret artwork without taking them out of the bag. The bags can be placed on tables so that the artists can create their artworks inside them.
3. After the artworks are finished, the artists should keep them hidden inside the bags. Don't put names on the artworks or the bags. Place the bags in the center of the room.
4. While the artists close their eyes, rearrange the bags.
5. The artists open their eyes and select a bag. They look at the artwork inside and try to match up the piece of art with the artist who made it.

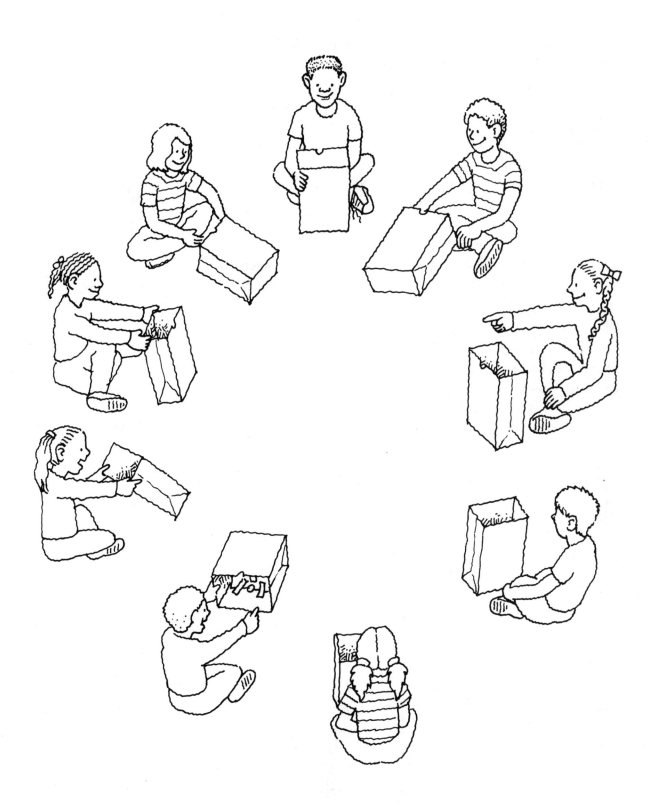

Critters

Thumbs up for these finger figures! A simple activity to introduce plasticine clay to tiny hands.

Materials

Plasticine (oil-based) clay
Pencils

Activity

1. Give each artist a small ball of clay—3 or 4 inches in diameter.
2. Instruct the artists step by step in how to make finger figures:

   - Roll the ball of clay into a flat cylinder.
   - Insert a pencil into one end of the cylinder to make a hole large enough to slip your finger into.
   - Stick the cylinder on your pointer finger.
   - Bend the top of the cylinder into a head.
   - Pinch each side of the back of the head for the ears.
   - With the point of the pencil, poke in two eyes and two tiny nostrils, and sculpt out a notch for a mouth.
   - With extra clay, add a unicorn horn, fins, teeth, arms, feet, and a tail.

3. Gather all the critters into the center of the room for a group dance and a parade—and then back into balls of clay until the next critter convention.

Gremlins

Gremlins have become infamous because these mischievous little elves can cause all sorts of impish problems. Be careful—they are about to invade the room and might create some unexpected disruptions!

Materials

Self-hardening clay
Pencils

Activity

1. Divide the self-hardening clay among the artists.
2. Instruct the artists step by step in the rare art of gremlin making:

   • Roll a lump into a cone shape with a flat base.
   • Create the ears by rolling two small, tapered cylinders.
   • Attach the ears to the cone-shaped body by poking two holes in the top with a pencil.
   • Insert the tapered cylinders into the holes and press them in firmly.

- Create a nose by rolling another tiny cone shape.
- Poke a hole into the center of the body and insert the tapered end of the cone into it.
- Smooth the clay together to attach it.
- Poke in some nostrils to complete the nose.
- Roll sausage shapes for the arms and legs and press them into the body.
- Use a pencil to carve round indentations for the eyes and a line for the mouth. (Some naughty gremlins even stick out their tongue.)

3. After the gremlins are finished, the artists find places to hide them around the room. What mischief can they get into? Gremlins can hang off lights, hide in bookcases, or rest under plants.

   The gremlins might eventually like a permanent home of their own, constructed from wood scraps and boxes. This way they won't pop up in unexpected places—and you can keep your eye on them!

Clay Play

A lump of clay may be the perfect metaphor for human creativity—in which "nothing" can be instantly transformed into something. Young artists press their imaginations into action as they add their personal touch to this malleable project.

Materials

Plasticine (oil-based) clay in various colors
Table covers
Plastic knives, forks, and spoons
Small objects such as paper clips, nuts and bolts, and popsicle sticks

Activity

1. Discuss a collective project to which the artists can each add their individual ideas. Select a theme that requires many elements to create the whole, such as a garden of flowers, a tray of pastry, or a farm yard filled with animals.

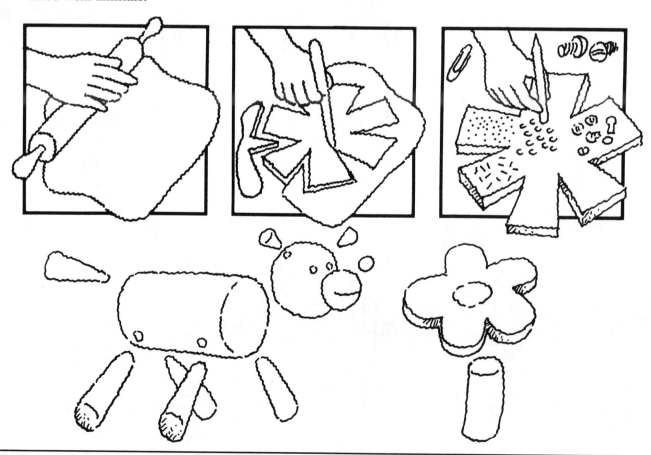

2. After the group has agreed on a theme, each artist is ready to contribute his or her own clay creation. Give each artist several balls of various colors of clay, approximately 2 inches in diameter.

3. At first, children will probably pound, punch, pull, and roll the clay into sausage shapes and mounds. Demonstrate some alternative techniques:

- Flatten balls of clay into slabs about half an inch thick. With a dull plastic knife, cut out shapes.
- Press textures into the surface with pencil points, nuts and bolts, paper clips, plastic forks, and other found objects.
- Expand three-dimensional forms by raising the shapes off the table with the addition of sides, legs, or stems.
- Roll out long, snakelike pieces. Connect them and coil them into a spiral to make bowls and cylinders.
- Reshape balls of clay by carving and cutting them with a plastic knife.

4. When the artists have all completed their part of the collaborative project, arrange the parts into a single display. A garden of flowers may need a clay fence, or a farm may need a barn. The group works together to make additional elements to complete their clay play.

Cast Party

Plaster has been used to make sculptures and frescoes for centuries. In the 15th century, when the gypsum used for its manufacture came from Montmartre, it became known as "plaster of paris." To this day, its versatility attracts artists young and old.

Materials

Plaster of paris (100-lb. bag)
Plastic food containers in various sizes and shapes
Plastic sandwich bags
Mixing container
Container of water
Newspaper and paper towels
Spatula

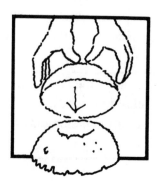

Activity

1. To control this messy material, organization is important. Cover the tables and floor with paper. Neatly arrange the plastic containers. Define one spot for mixing plaster.
2. The idea is to mold plaster into shapes in the plastic containers. Each artist works alone to experiment with his or her own personal ideas. Later, everyone will assemble the plaster pieces into one enormous sculpture.
3. Mix water into the plaster powder according to the directions. Add a little more water than needed so that the plaster will harden more slowly.

4. Although basic shapes can be molded in almost anything—such as cardboard tubes, paper cups, and egg cartons—plaster shapes can be formed most easily with plastic containers. Here are two techniques.

- **Cast Off.** Pour the plaster or shovel it with a spatula into a plastic container. Fill as many containers as you can as quickly as possible to any level. Let the plaster dry in the plastic molds. Free each plaster shape from its mold by popping it out as if it were an ice cube. If the shape is stuck inside the mold, slit the plastic with a utility knife to free the casting.
- **Squeeze Play.** Pour or shovel the plaster into plastic sandwich bags held by another artist. Tape the open end closed, mold the plaster by squeezing the bag into a free-form shape, and hold the bag until the plaster hardens. Flatten the bottom if a stable base is desired. When the plaster is set, peel away the plastic bag.

5. After plaster shapes are thoroughly dry, permanently attach them by adding more plaster between shapes. Artists work together to arrange the final sculptural shape. The sculpture might be constructed on a wooden base so that it can be moved easily. The completed sculpture may be painted with tempera paint.

Product Development

Thomas Edison, Henry Ford, and Alexander Graham Bell may be gone, but the spirit of American ingenuity lives on! It's the unflinching desire to make a better world through technology. New problems arise every day that need newfangled machines to solve them. Although these ideas for products may not actually work, they are a first step toward wonders of the future.

Materials

Cardboard cartons of various sizes, found objects, scrap materials
Spray paint
Tempera paint, containers, and brushes
Scissors
Construction paper
Stapler
Tape
White glue

Activity

1. List some inventions that are used every day, such as hair dryers, televisions, can openers, and battery-powered toothbrushes. Make a list of the benefits of each invention.

2. Make a list of problems for which no helpful invention exists. Then brainstorm solutions for each problem—serious or silly. Here are some examples.

   • Talking to your pet—"Animal-Talk Translator"
   • Lost articles—"Fast Finder"
   • Litter in the streets—"Instant Garbage Disintegrator"
   • Too short to see a parade—"Shoe-Ladder Lift"
   • Too cold, too hot—"Envir-o-matic Climate Control"
   • Being bored—"Party in a Minute"

3. Divide the group into research teams of two or three. Each team makes a model of its invention. Because the ideas are fanciful, the inventions need not actually work; they can just illustrate how they might appear. The teams construct models out of found objects and scrap materials.

4. After the models of the inventions are constructed, plan a trade show or a World's Fair display to show off the futuristic marvels. Each research team gets to describe its invention and how the product benefits the human race.

Supermarket

Grocery stores have rows and rows of brightly designed packages, all screaming for our attention. The power of advertising is used to try to convince us to buy one product rather than another. Young artists now turn the table and take control of their own packaging.

Materials

A sheet of poster board or oak tag for each artist
Pencils
Rulers
Metal straight edge
White glue
Tempera paint, containers, and brushes
Spray varnish

Activity

1. Assign the artists each to bring in an empty box from a household product, such as cereal, crackers, toothpaste, spaghetti, milk, or cleaning pads.
2. Give each artist a sheet of poster board or chipboard and a pencil. They can share rulers, metal straight edges, masking tape, and white glue.
3. Instruct artists how to make a cardboard pattern of the box of their product.

   • Carefully pull apart the original box to make a flat pattern.
   • Trace the pattern with a pencil.

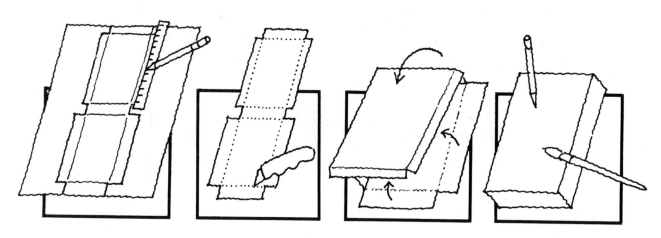

- Slightly enlarge the outline of the pattern to make a larger surface so that it will be easier to paint small details, such as lettering and pictures.
- With adult supervision, carefully use a utility knife to cut and score the pattern.
- Fold the pattern back into a box and neatly glue or tape it together.

4. Discuss the idea of adding a humorous twist to the product. For example, "Knits Crackers" (instead of Ritz)—the crackers that are knitted instead of baked—or "Flab" (instead of Fab)—the detergent for overweight clothes. Young artists invent their own visual and verbal puns or jokes about their product.

5. They sketch the artwork onto the box with a pencil, carefully imitating logos, layouts, and lettering. Direct them to neatly paint in the outlines with tempera paint. Supply small paint dishes to each artist so that colors can be mixed to match their product. After the boxes are finished, coat them with a spray varnish for added protection.

6. The group works together to create a supermarket display with their products. Get permission to use a display window at school or possibly a window in a neighborhood store. Request leftover advertisements from the local supermarket to enhance the effect and make the display look like a real supermarket.

Windowonderland

It might be called "art under glass." This window display is a public art project that takes the audience into consideration. Artists aren't selling a product, but rather new vistas for expression.

Materials

Cardboard boxes of assorted sizes
Flat sheets of cardboard
Colored construction paper
Scissors
Stapler
Duct tape
Tempera paint, containers, and brushes
Old magazines and collage materials

Activity

1. Take the group for a walk through the local shopping district to look at various window displays. Later, discuss design observations—what did they like, what was dull and boring, how were things constructed, and so forth.
2. The group searches for a window in which to create its own display. This might be a display cabinet at school or the window of an unoccupied store. (It might be better to try a test display in a familiar space before attempting one in a public window.) In all cases, you will need to secure permission to use the window from the person responsible for it, such as a school official or the building owner.

3. The group works together, sharing ideas and doing sketches of the window. Encourage design ideas to fit into the actual space. Artists should design something that will attract passersby. For example, everyone would be curious to peek into the window covered with paper in which there was a small hole under a sign that said "Don't Look!"

4. When designs are finished, production begins. Depending on the design, an assortment of materials will be needed, such as paper, paint, and cardboard. Utilize the lighting sources within the window, or include a special lighting source, such as clip lights or a string of holiday lights.

5. Install the window display and watch for reactions. Evaluate the various reactions and discuss alterations and ideas for future window wonders.

Aqua Art

Ahoy artists! Prepare your sea legs as this artwork sets sail for fun. It's not necessary to know fore from aft, because artists invent their own imaginative vessels.

Materials

Aluminum foil food containers
Styrofoam egg cartons and packing materials
Aluminum foil
Kitchen sponges
Cork
Plastic soda straws
Popsicle sticks
Plastic tape
Scissors
White glue
Stapler

Activity

1. The idea is not to make a boat but to make a sculpture that floats. Young artists should feel free to experiment with unconventional shapes. Divide the group into teams of two or three. Provide an assortment of materials that are likely to float, such as styrofoam, foil, cork, and sponges. Fill a small tub or tot pool with water.
2. To design the floating sculpture, each team begins with the base. An aluminum foil tray or styrofoam egg carton works well, or popsicle sticks can be glued together in a crisscross grid to make a raft.

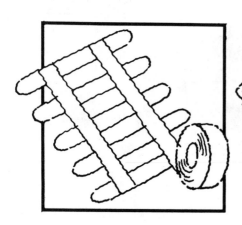  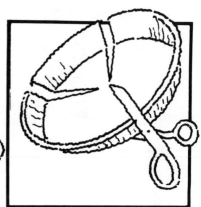

3. Each team works together to create a construction of shapes to go on the base. They can use plastic tape to construct a soda straw framework and cut out styrofoam shapes to attach to the framework. Or they can simply cluster sponges, foil, corks, partially inflated balloons, and other water-resistant objects into an assemblage.

4. The teams should periodically test their aqua art sculptures in the pool as they are constructing them. Adjustments will need to be made for balance and weight. In this project the artwork not only must look beautiful but it must remain afloat as well.

5. When the teams have completed their sailing sculptures, give each one a chance to officially launch its aqua art—with a title. Later, organize an aqua art parade or regatta.

Windfull

Although we can't see it, measure it, or weigh it, the wind fascinates us at any age. The wind is the secret ingredient that gives form to this air sculpture. Depending on how it blows, this artwork will flutter, flap, or sway in the breeze.

Materials

Bolt of fabric (fabric stores may donate or sell outdated stock at a reduced price)
Ribbons
Old clothes
Fabric scraps
Clothesline rope
Clothespins
Heavy twine
Scissors
Stapler
String
Felt-tip markers
Spray paint

Activity

1. Find an open field or playground with trees, a flagpole, fences, or other anchors to which the sculpture can be tied.
2. Tie the clothesline rope at each end of the field or playground, or crisscross the rope between trees.

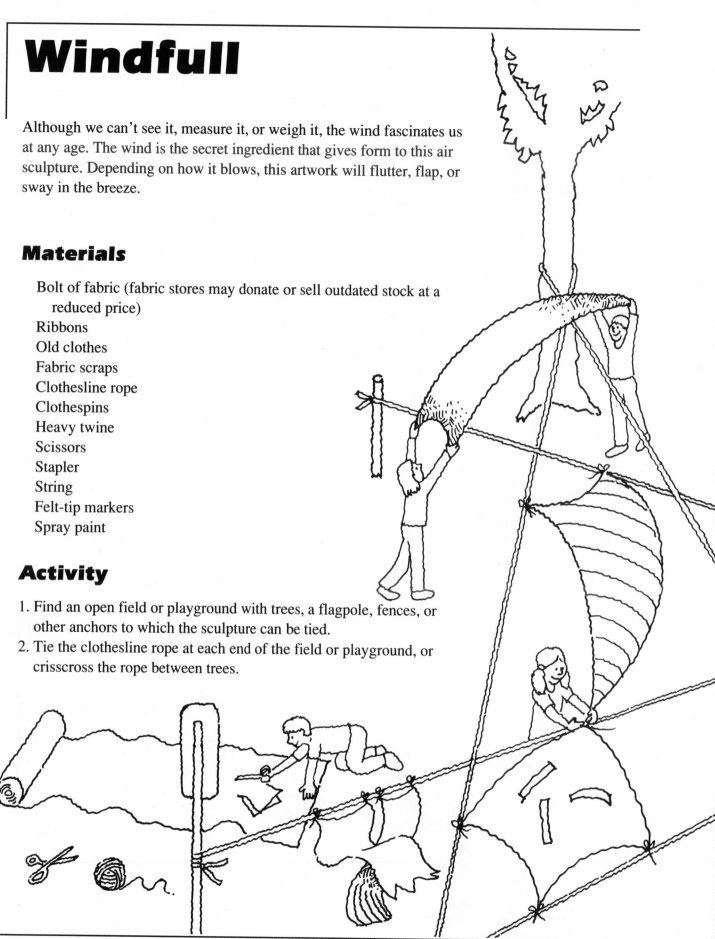

3. Roll a bolt of fabric across the ground. The artists cut the fabric into large shapes—round, zigzagged, free-form, curvy, anything!

4. Designs can be painted on the fabric shapes with felt-tip markers or spray paint. Artists may want to add patterns—such as stripes, checks, or dots—or pictures.

5. The artists tie one end of each fabric shape to the clothesline rigging with a piece of string, or clip the fabric on with a clothespin. Allow the fabric to inflate with the wind. String may be tied to the loose end of any shape through a small hole cut about 2 inches from the edge. Then the shape can be lashed to a tree or fence as it billows out. Artists may staple ribbons and other free-floating fringe to further show off the invisible force of the wind.

Variation

Tie an assortment of odd-shaped fabric pieces to a flagpole rope. Attach as many shapes as possible from top to bottom. As the wind changes, so will this tower of art.

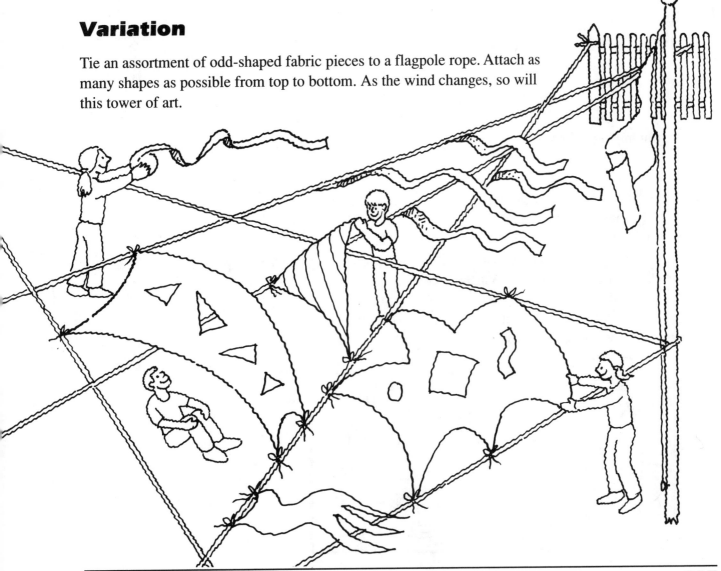

Balloon Platoon

Long before Orville and Wilbur took to the air, people were already floating around in hot-air balloons. In 1783 the Montgolfier brothers of France were the first people to fly in a balloon. Now the sport of ballooning is over 200 years old. Although these artists will remain earthbound, their imaginations will take off with this 8-foot model.

Materials

48 sheets of 20" x 30" tissue paper
8 feet of construction or kraft paper
Scissors
Masking tape
Rubber cement
Camping stove

Activity

1. No more than six or seven children should work on a single balloon—so you might want to build several. Before you present this activity to the young artists, enlarge the illustrated pattern on wrapping paper for them to trace.

2. Each balloon platoon of children joins four sheets of tissue paper end to end—making a strip 20 inches wide by 120 inches long—on which they will eventually trace the pattern. They overlap the edges of each sheet of tissue paper approximately half an inch, and glue the edges together with rubber cement to make secure seams.

3. Each balloon platoon makes 12 tissue paper strips and stacks them in a pile. The wrapping paper pattern goes on top, and all 12 strips are cut at once. Save the scraps for repairs.

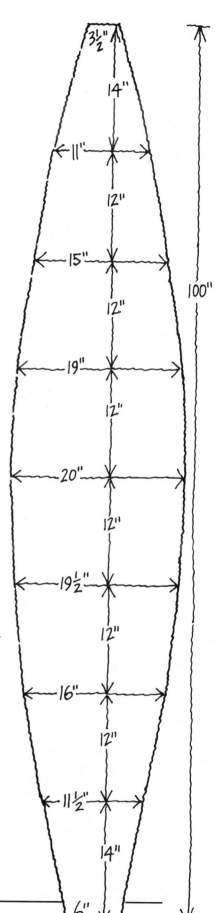

4. The balloon platoon carefully begins to glue the strips together—starting at the mouth, or wide end, and working up the curve to the small end. Patches and wrinkles are inevitable but will not affect the functioning of the balloon. The artists continue to glue all the strips together. They'll need to make sure they've glued all 12 before gluing the final seam.

5. When all the strips are joined into the balloon shape, there will be a small hole on top and a big hole, or mouth, on the bottom. The artists make a circular patch to cover the smaller hole—approximately 12 inches in diameter—and glue it on.

6. Then they form a tissue paper cylinder for the larger opening, or mouth, and fasten it to the balloon with masking tape. This will help to fill the balloon with hot air and provide stabilization in flight.

7. The balloon platoon decorates the balloon with bold, colorful designs, symbols, and words. Tissue paper shapes will not add too much weight to the balloon.

8. Prepare the launch area in a parking lot or open yard—free of trees, wires, and other obstacles. It is difficult to launch the balloon if it is windy; early mornings or late afternoons are usually calmest. Make a patch kit filled with masking tape, rubber cement, and tissue, and keep it handy.

9. Use a small camping stove to heat the air for the balloon. Carefully hold the mouth of the balloon above the heat. A group of balloonists should support the balloon over the heat as it inflates. This will take about 5 to 15 minutes.

10. When the balloon is fully inflated, have a countdown and release it. It will float up. As the air in the balloon begins to cool, it will slowly float down. Because balloons are unpredictable, however, it might travel high in the air or it might simply descend. Try several launches—but no matter how high the balloon flies, spirits are certain to soar!

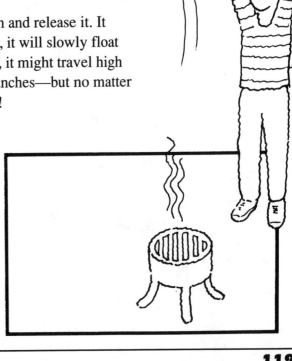

Scare Tactics

Maybe it's too horrible to believe, but the room has been invaded by a ghostly menace. It may pop up in the corner or fly across the room. Be prepared for some weird surprises.

Materials

Sheets of cardboard
Black yarn
Fabric scraps
Balloons
Paper
Tempera paint, containers, and brushes
Flashlights
Scissors
Masking tape

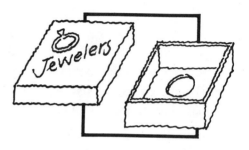

Activity

1. Make a list of some of the scariest things that group members can think of. The dark, thunder and lightning, strange noises, dead things—all the stuff that frightens them the most.
2. Talk about ways in which the group can turn the room into a scary place. They might create monsters, flying bats, and spooky sounds, for instance.
3. Divide the group into teams of three or four artists to create scary stuff. Here are some ideas.

- **Dead Finger.** Cut a hole in the bottom of a small gift box. Cover your finger with talcum powder and paint on bruises and a purple fingernail. Slip your finger through the hole in the box and put some cotton around it—and maybe drip on some ketchup for blood.
- **Eyeballs.** Peel some grapes and drop them in a bowl for a tactile surprise for blindfolded explorers.
- **Brains.** Chill a bowl of cooked noodles. Blindfolded players will be convinced that it's real.
- **Human Heart.** This unpleasant idea is made from a canned tomato dumped into a bowl.
- **Spooky Sounds.** Tape-record clanking chains, screams, witches' cackling laughter, creaky doors, and heavy thuds walking up a stair-case. If the tape recorder has a speed adjustment, play the sounds back on a lower speed.
- **Scary Sights.** On mural paper draw a backdrop of life-sized pictures of skeletons, ghosts, haunted houses, and flying bats.

4. Each team installs its horrible stuff in the room. Have artists arrange the room into a maze of horrors, through which each person will be led one by one. Some experiences will need blindfolds, but darken the room so that everyone will get good and scared. Later, when everyone is safe and sound, vote on the favorite fright.

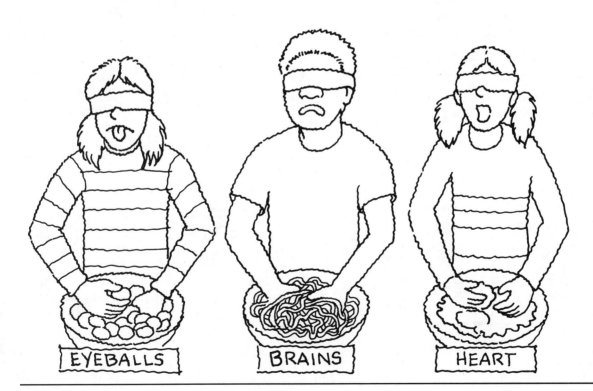

Castle Connection

Originally, castles were built to protect the people inside from outside invaders. Filled with tunnels, secret rooms, and lookout towers, this cardboard version promises to be a worthy fortress against invading adults.

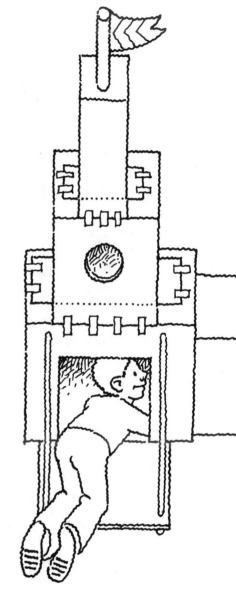

Materials

Lots of boxes (found at supermarkets, appliance stores, and
    department stores)
Utility knife
Silver duct tape
Steel ruler
Pencils
Tempera paint, containers, and brushes

Activity

1. Before the day of the project, ask each person to bring in a cardboard box. Ahead of time, start collecting additional boxes, cardboard tubes, and flat cardboard at local supermarkets and department stores, and store them away.
2. Discuss the idea of a castle. Bring in library books to show pictures of walls, towers, and slot-shaped windows.
3. Demonstrate ways to join boxes. To join two boxes of the same size, open the flaps on the ends of both boxes. Mesh the boxes together by putting the top flap of one inside and the top flap of the other outside and then alternating flaps inside and outside around the box. Tape the flaps in place with duct tape.

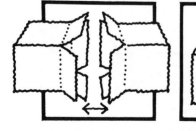 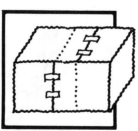 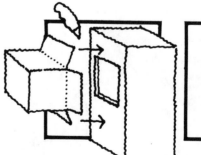 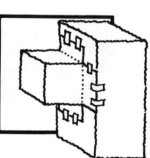

To join a smaller box to a larger, appliance-sized carton, use the utility knife to cut a hole in the larger carton the same size as the smaller carton. Tape the flaps of the smaller carton to the side of the larger one.

4. The artists now begin to design the castle. They may want to arrange boxes into shapes before the actual construction starts. Adult supervision of the utility knife will be necessary to cut out peepholes and lookout slots. But allow the castle to evolve into the shape it wishes.

5. After construction is completed, the artists may add to the fantasy by painting a stone pattern with tempera paint on the outside, attaching flags made of fabric scraps and colored construction paper, and finally adorning themselves as lords and ladies.

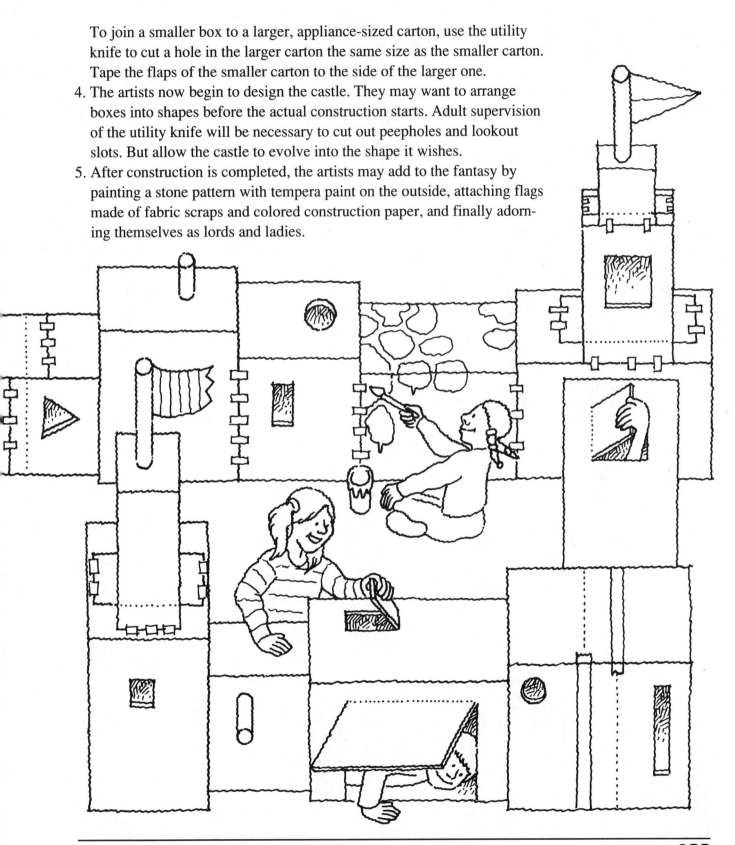

A Magic Nation

Just as Christopher Columbus bravely sailed across the Atlantic Ocean bound for some unknown land, young artists will have a chance to discover their own new world. Utopia might be unrealistic, but here's an opportunity to design a place that is as close to perfect as possible.

Materials

Large appliance cartons
Utility knife
Tempera paint, containers, and brushes
Pencils
Duct tape
Paper
Scrap materials

Activity

1. Describe to the group examples of totally planned cities, such as the following.

   • **Washington, D.C.** Designed by Pierre L'Enfant, this city is organized around a central pedestrian mall, with wide streets and planned vistas of monuments and government buildings.

   • **Brasilia.** The capital of Brazil was totally designed in the 1950s by Oscar Niemeyer. Each building has its own shape and character. The simple sculptural forms do not have any historic context but, rather, exist as modern works of art.

   • **Visionary Cities.** Architect Paolo Soleri has proposed enormous cities within one single complicated structure that contains everything their citizens need to live, work, play, and survive. Since 1970 he has been building a prototype of his ideas, which is called "Arcosanti," in Arizona.

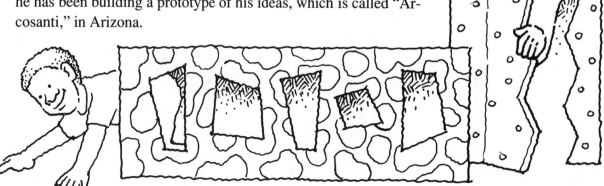

- **Broadacre City.** Designed by the famous American architect Frank Lloyd Wright, this was a model of his idea of the ideal community. Each person would live on an acre of land, and areas to work and places to play and shop would be interwoven throughout. Invite a city planner from the local government to describe some of the problems of designing an entire city.

2. Pretend that there aren't any restrictions for designing a city. Discuss some ways in which cities might be better or more fun. Artists can draw ideas with paper and pencils. This is an opportunity to brainstorm wild schemes. The artists pool their ideas and begin to agree on a basic direction for their design.

3. Divide the group into teams of two or three architects to build the city. Large appliance boxes can be transformed into fantasy architecture. (You will need to assist youngsters in cutting windows and doors with a utility knife. Have them mark cutouts in pencil so that you can slice the cardboard.) Surfaces can be decorated with tempera paint and collage materials.

4. As the structures are completed, the artists begin to landscape the room and position the buildings. Streets and paths can be created with children's building blocks.

   When everything is in place, gather everyone together for the official opening ceremonies. Give the city a name and elect a mayor to cut the ribbon!

Variation

For smaller spaces, young architects can create a model city with cereal boxes, milk cartons, shoe boxes, and other small objects.

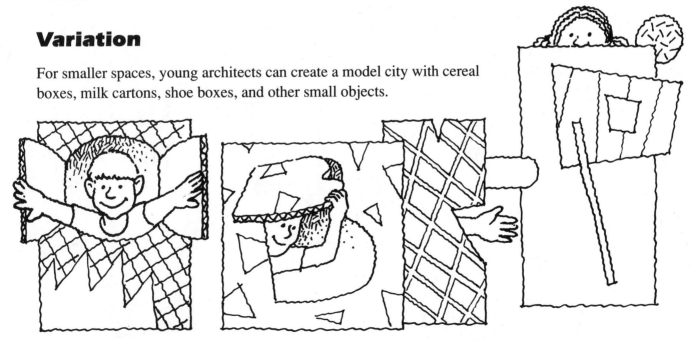

Monument to Us

All great societies like to leave structures as enduring legacies of who and what they are. The Egyptians have the pyramids, the Greeks have temples, and the Chinese have their Great Wall. Washington, D.C., is chock-full of monuments—from the Lincoln Monument to the Vietnam Veterans' Memorial. Now your group will build a lasting tribute to itself.

Materials

Cardboard boxes
Scrap materials, such as styrofoam, wood, paper
White glue
Masking tape
Duct tape
Tempera paint, containers, and brushes
Utility knife
Pencils

Activity

1. Discuss ways in which historic moments and heroic people are remembered through architecture and sculpture. The architecture might be as unusual as the St. Louis Arch or the Statue of Liberty.

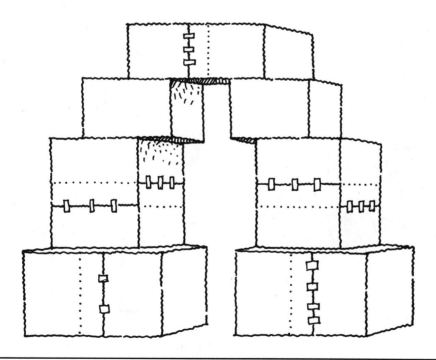
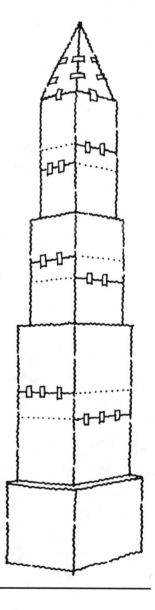

2. The group designs a shape for its monument. It might be an obelisk or totem pole, a pyramid or dome, or a simple wall or arch. Words and pictures on the monument might also help define it.

3. After the artists agree on a shape, they work together to build it. They can attach boxes with silver duct tape, glue 3-D relief (styrofoam, wood, and other scraps) to the surface, and then unify the surface with paint and images.

4. When the monument is complete, organize an official dedication ceremony. After the unveiling, you can be certain that the group will never be forgotten.

Time Exposure

A time capsule is an attempt to capture a moment in time and send it out into the unknown future. Small mementos are charged with our common experiences. When this artwork is opened months—or years—from now, the group will see how they've changed—or stayed the same.

Materials

Old suitcase or wooden box
Paper
Pencils
Tempera paint, containers, and brushes
Tape
Scissors
Magazines and assorted timely media

Activity

1. A time capsule is a record of the group. It could include drawings, objects, mementos, photographs, tape recordings—anything that would show who was in the group and what they were like. Discuss the kinds of things that might be included.
2. Select a container for the memorabilia. It might be a heavy-gauge cardboard box, a wooden box, or an old suitcase.

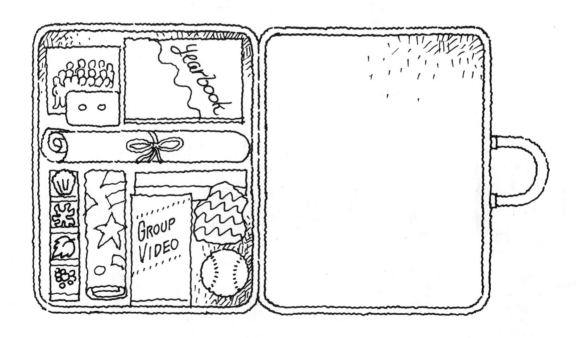

3. Create things to fit in the time capsule. Flat pictures, for example, don't take up much space. Include a few special objects—a baseball used by the group, a yearbook, a favorite magazine—but keep them small. The group might also want to tape-record their predictions for the future.

4. When the time capsule is filled, seal it and affix a label with the date it was closed and the date it should be opened. Store it away in a place where no one will be tempted to peek prematurely. Arrange to open it while the group is still together. If this is a school class, it could be in a few years. If it's not, you may open it in a few months.

Skyworks

A perfect finale for any celebration, this air art flows freely with a life of its own. In this project, art merges with meteorology as wind, temperature, and gravity have an effect on this buoyant sculpture.

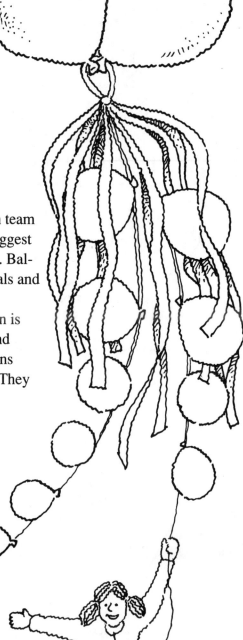

Materials

A tank of helium
Balloons of various sizes—14" to 40"
Crepe paper streamers
Surveyor's flagging ribbon (from the hardware store)
Plastic sheets
Plastic bags
Nylon twine
Transparent tape
Stapler

Activity

1. Divide the group into skyteams of five or six artists each. Each team designs a skywork with the lightweight materials available. Suggest that they keep the designs simple and in an open configuration. Balloons filled with helium provide the lift, and the plastic materials and the streamers provide the spatial qualities of the design.
2. Skyteams work indoors to lay out their sculptures. Construction is basic cutting, taping, and stapling of plastic shapes, ribbons, and streamers. The teams need to decide how and where the balloons should be attached to give their sculptures both lift and shape. They also need to choose a color scheme, sizes, and positioning.

3. Before launch time, the skyteams inflate balloons with helium and attach them to their skyworks. It is a good idea to tether the sculptures indoors in order to make final adjustments, such as adding more or larger balloons and altering balloon positions. Then the teams can attach streamers and other decorations.

4. When the skyworks are ready to launch, the skyteams carefully take them outdoors. They'll need to replace any popped balloons. (On very hot days, underinflate the balloons.) Then each team ties strings to several points and extends its skywork into the air, seeing how high the sculpture will go without getting caught in a tree or tangled on a lightpole. The teams tie their skyworks to a flagpole, a fence, or some other anchor so that everyone can enjoy the air art. Discourage skyteams from releasing their sculptures into the air because they will add to the global skyworks litter problem. Instead, see which skywork stays aloft the longest.

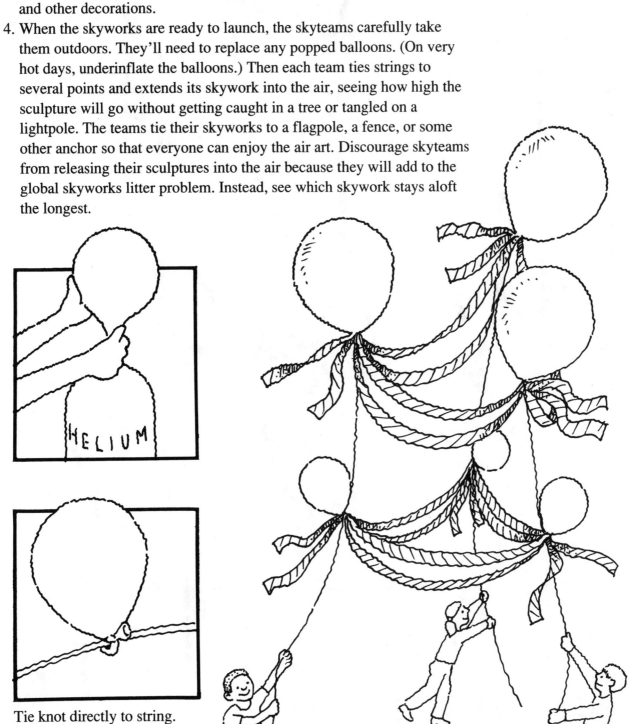

Tie knot directly to string.

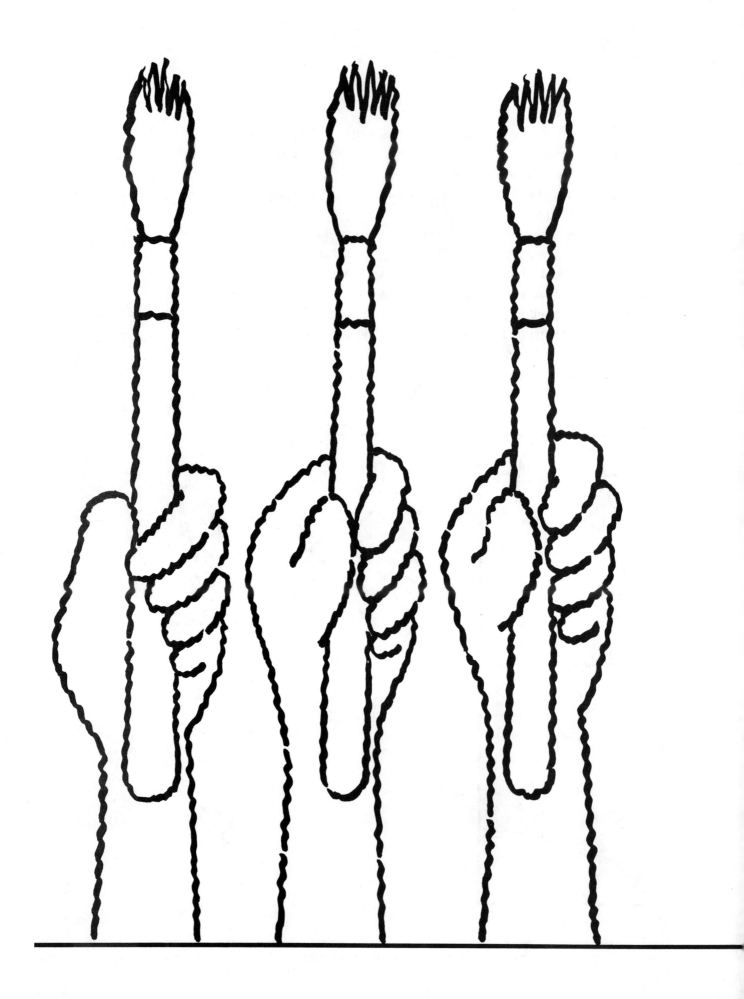

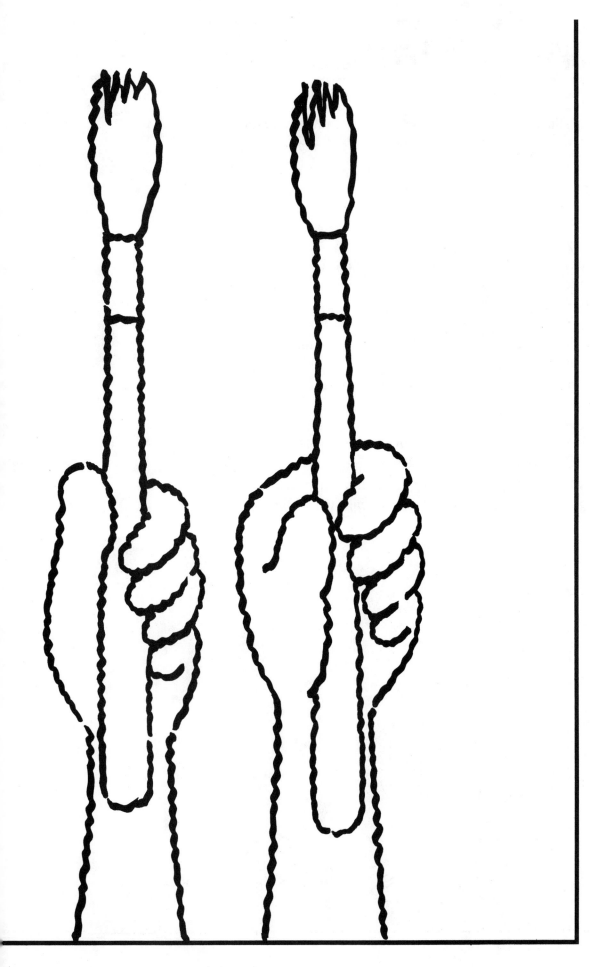

MURAL IN IN ONE

Drawing Dance

Two different disciplines come together to create a new art form. Artists will toe the line as they do felt-tip marker mambos and pencil pirouettes.

Materials

Roll of mural paper
Pencils, felt-tip markers, or crayons
Tape recorder or record player and an assortment of music

Activity

1. Roll out the mural paper across the floor. Artists remove their shoes and socks.
2. Give each artist a pencil, a felt-tip marker, or a crayon. Have the artists slip the drawing implement between their toes.
3. Select a variety of musical styles—slow waltz, jazz, Latin, pop.
4. When the music begins, the artists move their feet to the beat. Artists dance between and around each other without bumping.
5. As the artists become better at the drawing dance, have them add a second drawing implement between their toes. Change the rhythm of the music to see if the lines and shapes will change.

Doodle-lee-doo

It may not be the pulse of the art world, but drawing to the beat of this musical mural can add the right rhythm to any design.

Materials

Roll of mural paper
Felt-tip markers or crayons
Record player or tape recorder and upbeat music

Activity

1. Roll out the mural paper across the floor, leaving walking space all around.
2. Select music that has a distinct rhythm and an upbeat melody.
3. The activity is based on musical chairs. When the music begins, each artist selects a colored marker or crayon and draws a design inspired by the music.
4. When the music stops, the artists put down their markers and crayons and walk around the paper.
5. When the music begins again, the artists grab whatever marker or crayon is in front of them and add to the design that happens to be in front of them.
6. The artists continue to change places and switch designs whenever the music stops, until the mural is filled.

Variation

Try this activity with other media, such as watercolors, collage, or clay.

Just a Minute!

The pressure is to add to this work in progress. Stash it out of sight until permission is given for another 60 seconds of speedy spontaneity.

Materials

Roll of adding machine paper, approximately 4" wide
Pencils, felt-tip markers, crayons, or other drawing tools
Rubber bands

Activity

1. Cut strips from the roll of adding machine paper. To determine the length of each strip, divide the length of the entire roll by the number of artists in the group. Roll up each strip and secure it with a rubber band.
2. Give each artist a roll of paper and drawing implements.
3. The idea is to occasionally give artists 60-second periods when they can unroll their papers and add to the drawings. These periods can happen throughout a day, a week, or a year, depending on how long you will be working with the group and how long the paper strips are. Artists should be prepared with an idea at a moment's notice.

4. After each period, artists roll up their papers and randomly trade them with one another. During the next 60-second period, artists might want to react to the last drawing or just add something totally unrelated. Each drawing is the spontaneous expression of the artist. The drawings can be pictures of people, places, dreams, designs, or a visual diary of activity. No one will ever know exactly how any drawing will turn out.

5. This is not a contest for the fastest drawing or the most paper covered. In fact, the artists might want to take their time in order to think about what to add. When the drawings are eventually finished, collect the strips and tape them back into a single roll. The final unveiling—or unrolling— might be straight down a hallway or across a playground, as the collective spontaneity is finally revealed.

Drips and Drabs

A painting party without paintbrushes! Artists use an assortment of non-art tools to discover new routes to self-expression.

Materials

> Sheets of paper
> Roll of mural paper
> Tempera paint
> Disposable pie tins or styrofoam trays
> An assortment of unconventional art tools, such as Q-tips, combs, soda
>   straws, string, and popsicle sticks

Activity

1. To begin, each artist experiments on his or her own sheet of paper. Supply an assortment of unusual art tools and disposable pie tins filled with tempera paint. Water down the tempera paint to a watercolor consistency.
2. Encourage artists to experiment with their non-art tools.

   - **String.** Dip the string into paint. Lift it out of the paint, holding both ends. Carefully drag the string across the surface of the paper.
   - **Comb.** Dip the teeth of the comb into the dish of paint. Place the comb on the paper and twist it from side to side.
   - **Soda straw.** Capture a drop of paint by dipping one end of the straw into the paint and placing a finger over the other end. Hold the straw over a piece of paper and remove your finger to release the drop of paint. Take another straw and blow the paint across the paper.

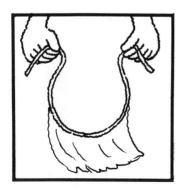 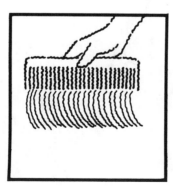 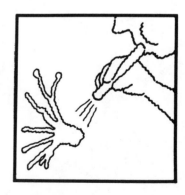

- **Q-tips and popsicle sticks.** Dip the cotton swab or stick into paint and experiment with ways to draw with it.
- **Sponge.** Dip the sponge into paint, squeeze out the excess paint, and dab it onto paper.

3. After the artists have experimented with various techniques, they are ready to work collaboratively on the mural. Roll out the mural paper across the floor. Artists weave their techniques together into a single sheet of colorful swirls. The more skilled that artists become with their offbeat tools, the less they may want to use an old-fashioned brush again!

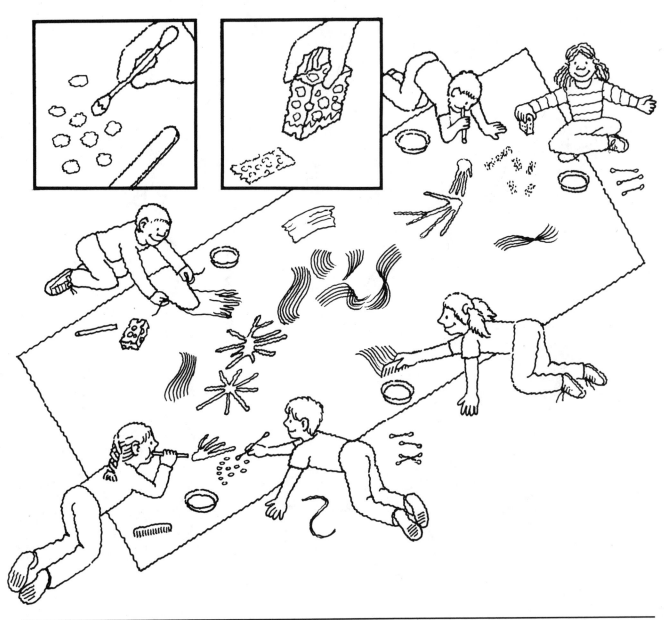

Michelangelo

Michelangelo never complained, but it must have been difficult to paint the Sistine Chapel ceiling while lying on his back, balanced atop scaffolding. This project shares some of the same problems—but although it may be over their heads, it's not out of the reach of young artists.

Materials

Mural paper
Masking tape
Felt-tip markers
Crayons
Pencils

Activity

1. Begin by discussing ceiling murals such as those of Michelangelo and other Renaissance artists. Many of these paintings incorporate the sky, clouds, and birds. Young artists may want to update the idea with space-craft, superheroes, and other contemporary sky images.
2. Since it's too difficult to draw on the ceiling, bring the "ceiling" closer by putting mural paper on the bottom of worktables. To attach the paper, turn each table over and tape it on.
3. Divide the group of artists into teams to work under separate tables. Each team designs its mural together.
4. While lying on their backs under the tables, the artists pencil in outlines of designs and fill in the outlines with markers and crayons.
5. After the ceiling murals are completed, each team takes a turn sliding under the other tables to see the finished products. The murals might then be mounted overhead, attached to the real ceiling.

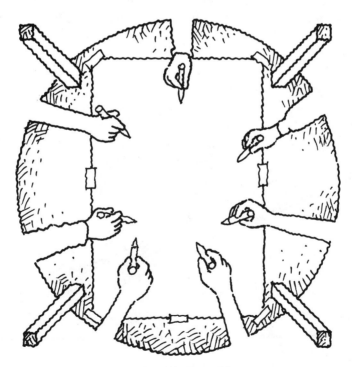

Underneath the table.

Dual Draw

The deal is two for one as artists try to master this double-tipped drawing. They may find that two pencils are better than one!

Materials

A roll of mural paper
Scrap paper
2 pencils per artist
Masking tape
Crayons
Felt-tip markers

Activity

1. Artists begin by experimenting on their own. Give each artist a sheet of paper, two pencils, and a piece of masking tape. Have some scrap paper handy for practice.
2. Show the artists how to make a dual-draw pencil. Hold both pencils together—side by side—in an upright position, and make sure that the points are aligned. Tape the pencils together.

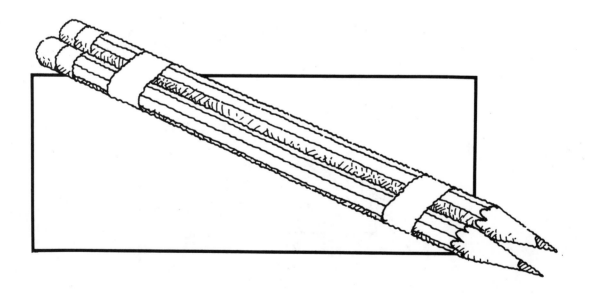

3. Then instruct the artists to begin to drag the pencils across a piece of paper, keeping the pencils upright in their drawing hand. They should apply equal pressure to both pencils while drawing. It will take some practice for young artists to make both pencils draw as one.

4. At first the artists can experiment with squiggles, loops, zigzags, and curves. Then they can try writing names and numbers.

5. When the artists feel confident, have them all draw together on a large sheet of mural paper. After the mural has been covered with double designs, they can fill it in with crayons and felt-tip markers, defining the loops so that the mural looks as if it were blanketed with floating ribbons of color.

Shape Scape

Shapes are all around us, right at our fingertips. This mural project makes visible those unseen shapes.

Materials

Roll of mural paper
Pencils
Felt-tip markers
Tempera paint, containers, and brushes
An assortment of objects that can be easily outlined, such as cups,
    spoons, stones, tape dispensers

Activity

1. Collect objects from around the room and place them in a pile. Roll out the mural paper across the floor and give each artist a pencil.
2. The artists each select an object to outline on the paper. (They should use pencils rather than markers or crayons, which will leave marks on the object.)

3. The idea is to fill the paper with outlined objects. Artists should try moving their objects around to new spots and angles and tracing them several times. They can also overlap other artists' objects.

4. After the paper is completely covered, the artists fill in the shapes with color. New outlines can be created by tracing with a marker around a combination of forms. Patterns, such as stripes, checks, dots, or squiggles, can be drawn within shapes. And areas can be colored in with paint, markers, or crayons.

5. After the shape scape is finished, the group has a record of the world around them through the creativity within them.

Blowup

Bigger may not necessarily be better, but it's certainly impressive. Enlarging a very small object can reveal some amazing details that are usually overlooked. Seeing will be sharpened as artists focus on every minute aspect.

Materials

Roll of mural paper
Pencils
Felt-tip markers or crayons
Magnifying glass

Activity

1. Each artist selects a very tiny object, such as a paper clip, a hairpin, a screw, a tweezer, a ring, or a wristwatch.
2. Roll out the mural paper on the floor. Each artist selects a space in which to draw an enlarged version of his or her object. Artists share the magnifying glass to study their objects. They should notice how different a surface appears close up, with irregular bumps and scratches.
3. Each artist pencils in the outline of his or her enlarged object as carefully as possible. Then surface texture, including any imperfections, can be added.
4. After everyone has finished, hang the mural of blowups on the wall. Each artist describes what he or she has discovered while closely examining the small sight.

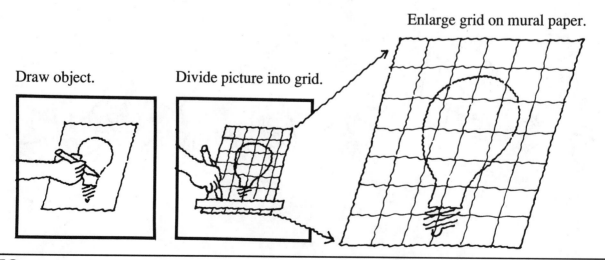

Draw object.   Divide picture into grid.   Enlarge grid on mural paper.

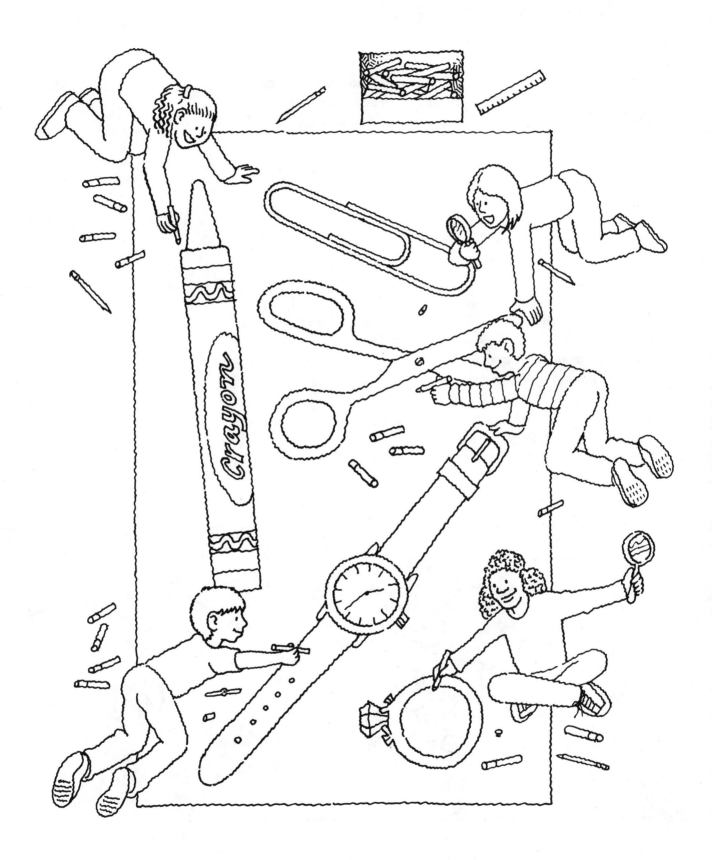

Chalk It Up

Art takes to the streets, sidewalks, buildings, and walls! Unlike graffiti, this outdoor art is intended to enhance the place in which it exists. It's public art for the passerby that expresses the environment as well as the artists.

Materials

A box of thin and thick pieces of chalk in various colors

Activity

1. Begin with a discussion about outdoor art such as murals, billboards, graffiti, and signs. Talk about how some fit into the landscape and how others do not. For example, a billboard advertising a giant bottle of soda might appear in a cow pasture, or a billboard showing a field of flowers might be in a city atop an office building.
2. Find a space in which to draw the chalk mural—a sidewalk, a street, or a concrete wall. Permission to use the space must be granted by the property owner. The rain will eventually wash the chalk mural away, so it will not permanently harm the surface.

3. The idea is to create a big chalk drawing that will visually fit into the surroundings. Young artists plan the design together. A small pencil drawing would help them to decide on the final concept. What will the image be? Should it blend into or comment on the surroundings? What will local people enjoy seeing?

4. Once a design has been agreed upon, artists outline the design. Later, they fill in the design with colors and details. Thick chalk works best for covering large surfaces.

5. After the mural is completed, ask for reactions from the neighbors. Collect ideas for future murals that might involve the participation of the people in the neighborhood.

Crayon and On!

Experimenting with art techniques can produce interesting effects. The versatile crayon offers a surprising range of possibilities.

Materials

Lots of crayons
Paper, corrugated cardboard, sandpaper, waxed paper, newspaper
Watercolor and tempera paint, containers, and brushes
Scissors
Popsicle sticks
Electric iron
India ink

Activity

1. To begin, each artist experiments alone with one or all of the following techniques.

   - **Classic Crayon.** Draw on different kinds of surfaces, such as cardboard, corrugated board, wood, and sandpaper. To color large areas, peel off the paper and rub the side of the crayon on the surface.
   - **Rubbing.** Peel the paper off the crayon. Select a few flat objects with textured surfaces, such as screens, leaves, rough sandpaper, corrugated board, or coins. Place a sheet of thin bond paper or newsprint over the object and rub with the flat side of the crayon. Switch textures and colors of crayons, overlapping the shapes and mixing the shades.

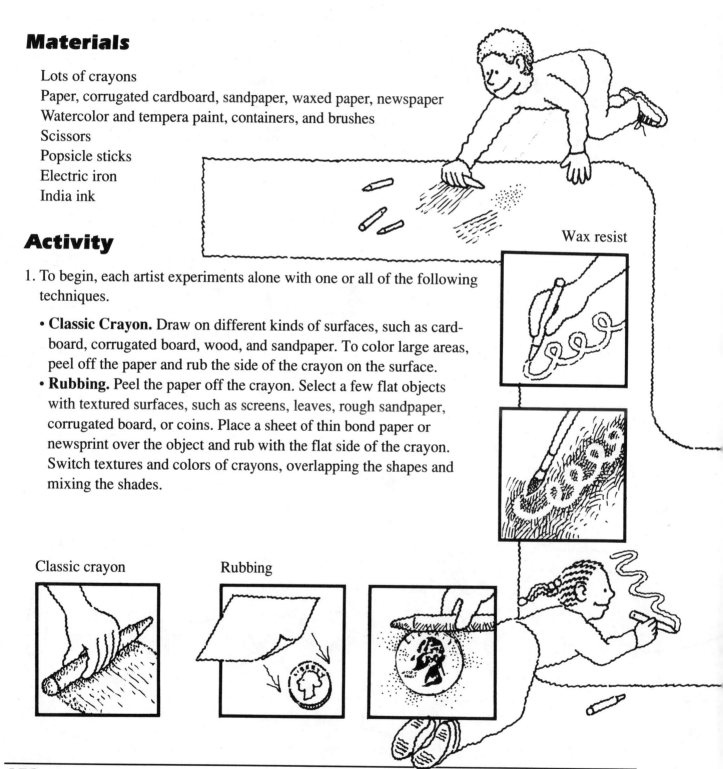

Wax resist

Classic crayon

Rubbing

- **Wax Resist.** Draw a design with a white or light-colored crayon on white paper. Draw over the lines several times to build up the wax. Next, brush watercolor or thinned tempera paint lightly over the crayon design. The color will not stick to the crayon; it will appear only on the paper. The design will appear as a negative image.
- **Encaustic.** Scrape shavings from crayons of various colors onto a sheet of waxed paper. A flat popsicle stick works well as a scraping tool. Place another sheet of waxed paper over the shavings. Place a sheet of newspaper over everything. Press the sheets together with a warm (not hot) iron. The crayon shavings will melt together into transparent colors.
- **Scratchboard.** Coat the paper with various colors of crayon, trying not to leave any of the paper showing. After the paper is completely covered with color, go over the entire surface with India ink or black crayon. After the ink dries, make a design by gently scraping into the surface with a pointed tool.

2. After artists have exhausted all routes of experimentation, have them cut the designs into shapes. The group arranges them into a gigantic collaborative design. Glue the shapes into a collage on a big sheet of paper.
3. Finally, have everyone work together to fill a large sheet of mural paper with the ultimate experimental crayon research project.

Scratchboard

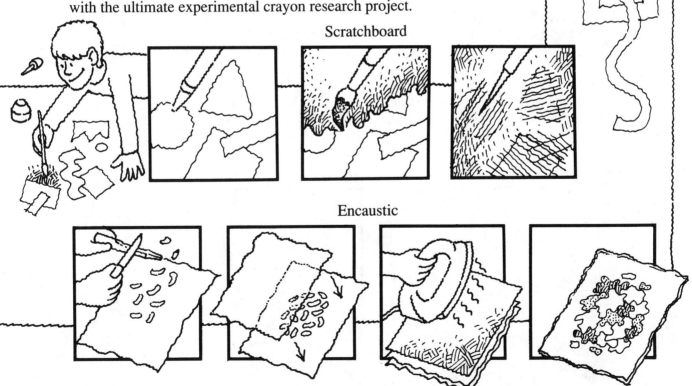

Encaustic

Print Mural Madness

Young artists will give their stamp of approval to this basic printing project.

Materials

Roll of mural paper
Tempera paint
Disposable pie tins or styrofoam plates
Brushes
Disposable objects, such as buttons, jar lids, old combs, corks, macaroni, plastic bottles, nuts and bolts

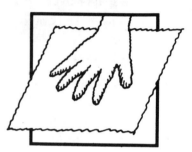

Activity

1. Roll out the mural paper across the floor.
2. Use pie tins for paint containers because they are flat and wide enough for dipping. Place one tin every few feet between the artists. Fill each tin with $1/8$" of tempera paint. Add a little water to give it a creamy consistency.
3. Give the artists an assortment of objects. They can either dip the objects into the paint or brush paint on them before they press them onto the paper. Painted fingers can also become part of the printed design.
4. Printing techniques that the artists can try include the following:

- **Handprints.** Place your hand on the paint in the pie tin. Then press your hand onto the mural paper and lift it off carefully to reveal the print.

Object prints

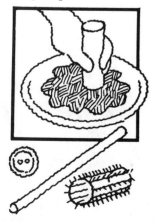
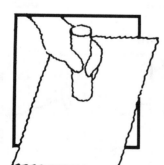
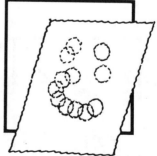

- **Potato prints.** Cut potatoes in half with a sharp knife. On the flat end of one of the halves, cut a simple shape, such as a circle, a triangle, or a square. Cut a different shape in each of the other halves for a set of potato printing stamps. Dip the potato stamp into the pie tin full of paint, and print it on the paper.
- **Object prints.** Use everyday items for instant stamps, such as buttons, paper clips, hair curlers, and plastic bottles. Dip the object in paint, and print.

5. Because the idea is to fill the paper with an enormous cooperative design, the artists should rotate around the paper to see if any areas need some extra printing. Encourage artists to design with the same object by doing repeat patterns, overlapping patterns, and patterns made by turning the object or placing it in different directions.

6. While the print mural dries, have artists clean up and wash their hands. Hang up the mural and discuss the impressions that printing has made on the group.

Potato prints

Picture Us

The artists will find their own niches in this life-sized group portrait. Body shapes become connected in this enormous string of full-scale cutouts.

Materials

A roll of heavy brown wrapping paper
Scissors
Pencils, crayons, or felt-tip markers
Tempera paint, containers, and brushes
Mirror

Activity

1. Roll out the brown wrapping paper across the floor.
2. Artists take turns lying face up on the paper. The idea is for artists to carefully trace around each person as accurately as possible. If the paper is as wide as the artists are tall, trace the outlines shoulder to shoulder, overlapping each one slightly. If the paper is too narrow to do that, trace the outlines as if each person were standing on the next person's shoulders.

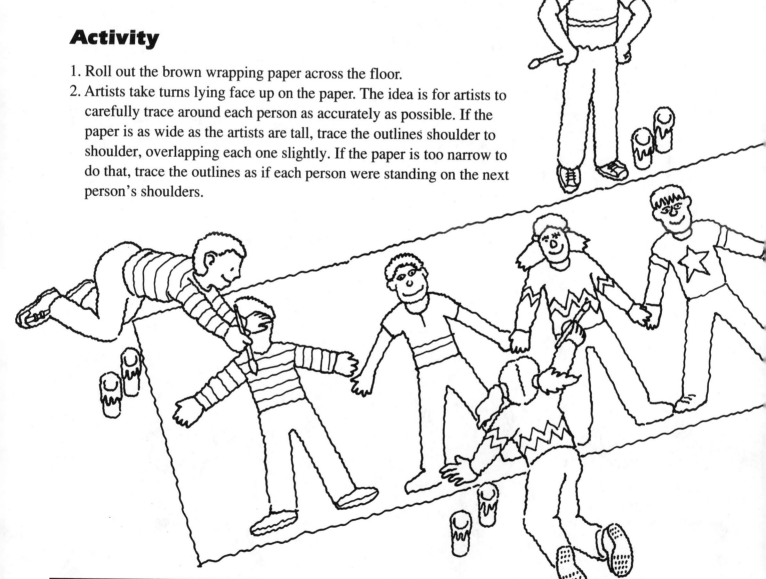

3. After everyone has been traced, each artist fills in his or her outline with a self-portrait. Encourage the artists to copy their clothes exactly. Have a mirror handy so that they can copy their faces, hair styles, eyes, and other features. Then they fill in the outlines with tempera paint.

4. When the paint has dried, instruct the artists to cut out the portraits, making sure that they remain connected with each other. Hang the string of portraits across a wall, or suspend it from the ceiling so that everyone appears to be flying over the room.

Royal We

Everyone gets to ascend the throne as they create their own royal group portrait.

Materials

Roll of mural paper
Pencils
Tempera paint, containers, and brushes
Assorted collage materials—sequins, foil, buttons, and so forth
White glue

Activity

1. The idea is to make a group portrait of the class, similar to a group photograph in which everyone stands together in several rows. Roll out the mural paper across the floor. The artists help each other trace their outlines in pencil. Everyone takes turns lying down to be traced. Overlap outlines so that everyone appears to be standing in rows and only heads and shoulders are visible.
2. The artists each add details to their own outline. Keep a mirror handy so that artists can check their features. Portraits need not be exactly accurate.
3. Show illustrations of kings and queens to the group. Research art history books and royalty. Artists select their favorite jewels, crowns, capes, high collars, and elaborate fabrics and incorporate them into their portraits.

4. Fill in outlines with brightly colored tempera paints. Artists may want to enhance the royal effects with glitter, glue, foil, and other shiny collage materials.
5. Paint in the background—maybe a castle or banners and other regal decor. Display the completed portrait in the royal gallery.

This royal group may be tempted to exchange stories about their life in the palace before today's modern conveniences.

Walkabout

Since each of us has different interests, different things catch our attention. We each experience a shared situation from our own personal vantage point. This project will help enlarge our vision and appreciate others' viewpoints.

Materials

Roll of mural paper
Pencils
Felt-tip markers or crayons
Tempera paint, containers, and brushes

Activity

1. Take the group for a short walk around the block, playground, or building. Instruct everyone to carefully observe things around them—facades, windows, trees, gardens, fences, anything seen while walking.

2. After the walk, roll out the mural paper across the floor. The idea is for the group to work together to reproduce the entire walk as accurately as possible from memory. The artists begin at one end of the paper and draw with pencil everything they remember seeing. To give the mural an overall structure, the leader draws a sidewalk or path across the paper to define the route, and then the artists and the leader work together to define notable landmarks and divide the walk into smaller sections.

3. The artists confer with one another and fill in as many tiny details as possible. They should try to recall the shapes of buildings and the designs of windows and architectural decoration. What kind of flowers were in the garden? Was there a birdhouse in the tree? Then they fill in the outlines with tempera paint or markers, trying to remember the proper colors.

4. After the mural is completed, the artists take the same walk again. This time they will compare reality with the product of their combined perceptions. You might call it a "walk down memory lane."

World Tour

A tour around the world takes a lot of planning, and this is no exception.
Artists will research various cities in order to organize their trip.

Materials

Roll of mural paper
Tempera paint, containers, and brushes
Pencils

Activity

1. Divide the group into a team for each city on the tour. The cities might
   be New York, London, Paris, Rome, Cairo, Moscow, and Hong Kong
   or whatever other cities the group selects.
2. Each team is responsible to research its city. The teams learn how the
   people dress, what types of jobs they do, what kinds of food they eat,
   and what the typical style of architecture is. What makes the city
   different from any other in the world?
3. Roll out the mural paper across the floor. Divide the paper equally
   among the tour teams. The teams arrange their cities across the paper
   in order of the tour.
4. Each team draws, paints, and adds collage cutouts to depict its city.
   For example, London might include drawings of Big Ben, Bucking-
   ham Palace, and a double-decker bus.
5. The picture of each city should include a means of transportation to
   it—boat, plane, car, or whatever. When the mural is finished, hang it
   across the wall. Each team takes turns giving a tour of its city.
   Don't forget your passport!

Circus Parade

It can't be beat! The popularity of the circus spans generations. From the old-time tents to the modern age of civic arenas, one thing has never changed—the circus parade!

Materials

Roll of mural paper
Tempera paint, containers, and brushes
Pencils
Scissors
Tape

Activity

1. Explain how circus performers used to parade through small towns to promote the show. List the types of performers that might be included, such as jugglers, fire-eaters, clowns, acrobats, weight lifters, stilt-walkers, animal trainers, elephants, and even a person being shot out of a cannon.
2. Divide the group into teams of two or three artists. Each team selects one or two performers to depict.

3. Roll out the mural paper. Cut a large sheet for each team. The teams draw outlines of their performers in pencil, making the images as big and detailed as possible.
4. They fill in the outlines with brightly colored tempera paint and decorate the performers' costumes with playful dots, stripes, and other patterns.
5. The teams cut out the completed pictures with a scissors and arrange the cutouts across the floor in the order in which they appear in the parade.
6. Roll small pieces of masking tape into loops to create two-sided adhesive. Stick the tape on the back of the cutouts and attach them to a wall. Add a little circus music—and on with the show!

3-D Daydream

Daydreams are fanciful thoughts that invade our minds while we are wide
awake. When we get bored, we can simply leave reality and get lost in
Walter Mitty notions of adventure or fun. It isn't every day, however,
that an entire group can agree to escape into the same daydream.

Materials

Roll of mural paper
Tempera paint, containers, and brushes
Construction paper
Masking tape
Scissors
Flat cardboard and assorted scraps
Felt-tip markers
Pencils and paper
Jigsaw

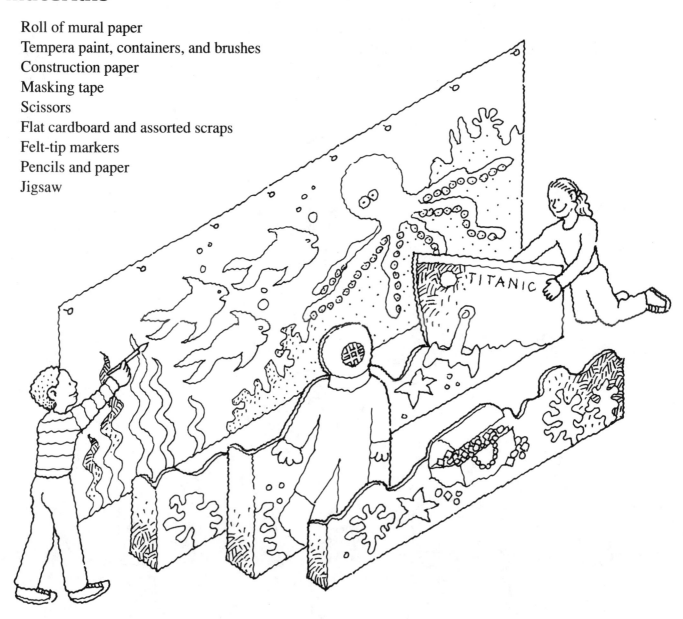

Activity

1. Everyone secretly writes two favorite daydreams on a piece of paper. The papers are folded and collected in a box. Read the daydreams out loud and list them on a big sheet of paper. Group similar daydreams into categories.

2. The goal is to come up with one big terrific daydream that everyone can agree on. Vote on which ones are favorites. Then try to incorporate as many different ideas as possible into one dream.

3. When a daydream is agreed upon, it's time to begin to design how it might be re-created in 3-D form. Dioramas are 3-D murals that incorporate foreground, middle ground, and background—sort of like the dioramas in natural history museums with stuffed animals and fake trees in front of a painted scene.

4. Divide the group into three diorama production teams. The "background" team creates a scenic 2-D mural. Those who like to build join the "middle" and "foreground" teams to construct 3-D models. All teams work together to blend color, scale, and composition.

5. The daydream comes true as the group assembles the pieces of the diorama. Add some spotlights for a more theatrical effect.

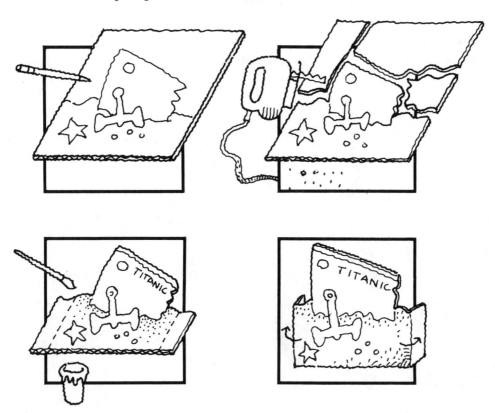

Air Strips

Fasten your seat belts! The artists are ready to take off with this high-flying outdoor floating mural.

Materials

Rolls of adding machine paper, about 3" wide
Scissors
Tempera paint, containers, and brushes
Felt-tip markers
Strong string or twine
Balloons
A small tank of helium with a regulator

Activity

1. Roll out a strip of adding machine paper along the ground. Place paint, brushes, and felt-tip markers every few feet between the artists.
2. Instruct the artists to fill in the thin strip of paper with drawings and designs—pictures, shapes, patterns, and so forth. Encourage the artists to think about pictures of things that are long and thin, such as a snake, a train, or a parade.
3. Once the strip is chock-full of images, begin to inflate a bouquet of balloons with helium. (Sometimes you can find giant 40" balloons in novelty shops.)

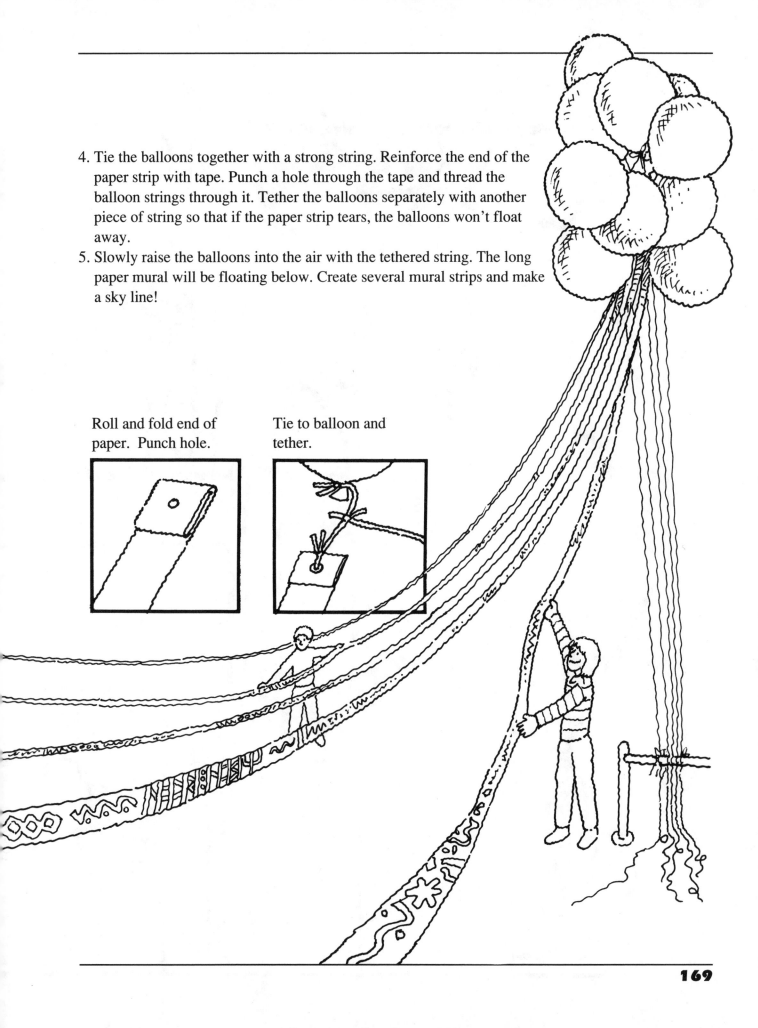

4. Tie the balloons together with a strong string. Reinforce the end of the paper strip with tape. Punch a hole through the tape and thread the balloon strings through it. Tether the balloons separately with another piece of string so that if the paper strip tears, the balloons won't float away.

5. Slowly raise the balloons into the air with the tethered string. The long paper mural will be floating below. Create several mural strips and make a sky line!

Roll and fold end of paper. Punch hole.

Tie to balloon and tether.

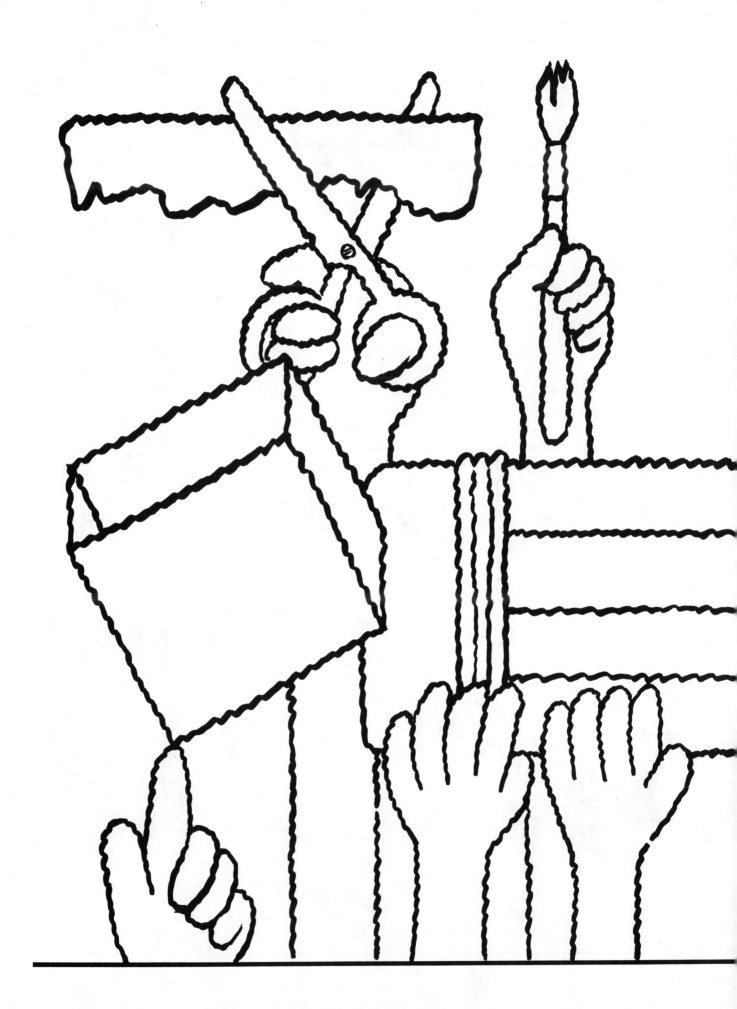

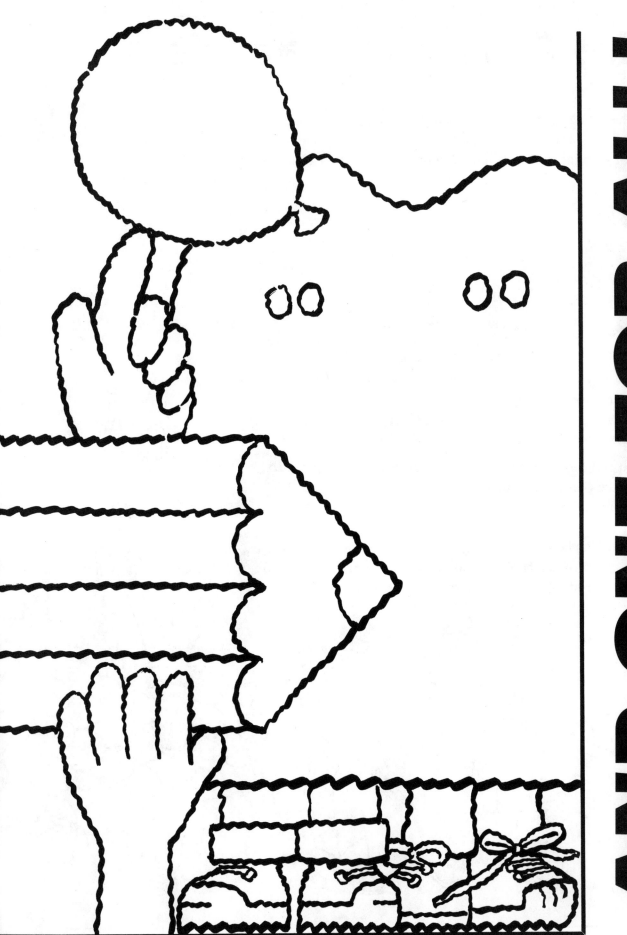

AND ONE FOR ALL!

Take Part Art Parade

Now that the young artists have worked together to create pictures, prints, murals, and sculptures, they are ready for an artful finale. Parades are a way of showing pride and spirit, but this parade is also a walking work of art.

Materials

See Take Part Art projects

Activity

1. Discuss with the group the idea of parades. Have them describe parades that they have seen and the floats, bands, and performers that they have enjoyed.
2. Review some of the projects in this book that might be included in a parade. For example,

   • Betwixt and Between can become a three-person clown act,
   • Mad Hatters can connect marchers with one hat,
   • Quick-Built Quilt can become banners and flags,
   • Multi-Masks can be worn by a choreographed dance group,
   • Perplexing Puppets can be enlarged into enormous abstract puppets,
   • Monument to Us can become a float constructed on a wagon, and
   • Together We Stand can be an enormous group costume finale.

3. Select various Take Part Art projects and divide the group into teams to work on each one. The size of the teams depends on the project—some may be three artists, while others may be six or more.

4. Review this book for directions and create the projects.

5. When parade elements are finished, the group organizes itself into a parade. Choreograph the parade so that it has a beginning, a middle, and an end. Flags and banners are a nice way to start the parade—and floats and big costumes are best as a spectacular finish. Artists can add sound with drums, rhythm sticks, or a portable radio or a tape recorder with marching music.

6. Notify the neighborhood or school of where and when the parade will happen. Strike up the band—and celebrate the group's collective creativity.

About the Author

As an artist and designer, Bob Gregson has created innovative programs for people of all ages. He's directed the art classes for the Wadsworth Atheneum in Hartford, Connecticut, taught at the Young Artists Studios in Chicago, and designed participatory programs for the Art Institute of Chicago and the Capital Children's Museum in Washington, D.C. In Hartford, Bob designed large-scale community festivals, such as Play Day and Thursday Is a Work of Art. As Special Events Director for New Haven's Department of Cultural Affairs, he directed the City's 350th birthday and produced New Haven Celebrates New Haven for 200,000 people. Bob is also the author and illustrator of the *Incredible Indoor Games Book* and the *Outrageous Outdoor Games Book*.